The Mystery of Woman

A Book for Men

The Mystery of Woman

A Book for Men

Gabriel Morris

Winchester, UK
Washington, USA

First published by Soul Rocks Books, 2012
Soul Rocks Books is an imprint of John Hunt Publishing Ltd., Laurel House, Station Approach,
Alresford, Hants, SO24 9JH, UK
office1@o-books.net
www.o-books.com

For distributor details and how to order please visit the 'Ordering' section on our website.

ISBN: 978 1 78099 359 1

A CIP catalogue record for this book is available from the British Library.

Design: Stuart Davies

Printed and bound in the USA by Edwards Brothers Malloy

We operate a distinctive and ethical publishing philosophy in all areas of our business, from our global network of authors to production and worldwide distribution.

CONTENTS

Introduction

Women have long been an enigma to men: shrouded in mystery, misunderstood, both desired and repressed, fought over, respected, honored, denied, manipulated, deified, veiled, lusted after, romanticized in countless songs and works of art and, at the very least, always keeping men scratching their heads in befuddlement.

This book is an attempt to pull away the veil, remove some of the mystery and give a glimpse into women's inner workings, desires, needs, visions, dreams, perspective, wisdom, creativity and everything else that encompasses the feminine being. It covers a variety of subjects that could hardly be more wide-ranging, tackling challenging topics from the repression of women and sexual inequalities, to tantra and sex magic; from the role of emotions in both women and in relationships, to trust, intimacy and communication; from the various shortcomings of men in relating to women, to the power of the penis, the true qualities of manhood and the importance of finding balance between masculine and feminine, yin and yang.

The book is a synthesis of writings from many different angles and varying points of view. Many are explicitly personal, whereas others come from a more professional perspective on relationships. The point isn't to tell the reader unequivocally: "this is the way it is". Because when it comes to relationships, there is no single, simple right answer. Instead, the multiple perspectives contained herein will open up the possibilities, open up the mind and heart and give a great deal of valuable information for men to work with when it comes to navigating the tricky waters of relationships.

In Part 1, drawing from my own romantic relationships and other interactions with women, I share my thoughts and insights on the ongoing struggle by men to relate with and genuinely connect with women; whether it means understanding, controlling, fighting, finding balance with, learning from, surrendering to or simply loving them as they are, mystery unsolved. I attempt to find that elusive balance between acknowledging some of the stark realities—that men have mistreated and suppressed women much more than the other way around—and delving into the true potential that exists in genuinely loving relationships between the sexes.

In Part 2, twenty-four different women tell their points of view in their own words and share their very personal thoughts and stories as they discuss everything under the sun when it comes to what they desire in relations with men. This is where the rubber hits the road, so to speak, and men will get an in-depth and totally unvarnished view of what women really want, what they need, what they think and how they truly feel about the complex realm of relationships, love, romance, sexuality, spirituality, the Goddess energy, the real roles of men and women, and much more.

And in Part 3, eight men share their experiences, thoughts and insights on relating with women and all of the above-mentioned subjects, as well as what it really means to be a man in the world today—treading that fine line between retaining one's masculinity, honoring the feminine both without and within, and searching for a new way of relating and being that embodies both the sensitive lover, and the triumphant spirit of the warrior.

The purpose of this book is not to simply be an interesting, perhaps titillating read. And I doubt most readers will experience it that way. Instead, it is meant to help change and transform at some deeper level men's views of women, relationships, sexuality, gender roles and the true potential of both manhood and of womanhood.

Our world has been in a state of imbalance for some time, in which men have ruled and dominated women, and in so doing have distorted both women and themselves. In short, the power of women, of the Goddess, has been subjugated. But both women and men have lost something valuable as a result. What better way to straighten things out, than to hear what women really have to say?

I'm certain that in the course of reading this book, men will find women's voices and the messages contained within them not only interesting and revealing, but also deeply thought-provoking and inspiring, for men to begin creating much deeper and more rewarding relationships with the women in their lives.

Part 1:

Yin vs. Yang?

Chapter 1

Make Love not War

At first glance this might seem a silly expression, as nonsensical as "Make Forks, Not Umbrellas". What does one necessarily have to do with the other? And yet on a deeper level (beyond it being simply an excuse to have lots of sex) it actually captures perfectly the solution to many of the world's chronic problems.

Men have been warring with one another for thousands of years. To some extent, women have joined in the fight and fought along with them, or at least supported their efforts. But the wars are almost always of men's making. Because the choice to go to war as a solution is part of the imbalanced, dominant male construct that has reigned for thousands of years on Earth and continues to permeate our modern-day societies. There are many different, seemingly practical reasons for waging war: territorial disputes, lack of food, water or other resources, lingering feuds, money, expanding power, disarming perceived threats, political rivalries and the list goes on.

But at the core of men's thirst for war, whether between nations, businesses, individuals or in a myriad of other forms, is a lack of connection with feminine love in the male psyche. People—men or women—don't inflict harm needlessly on others when they're connected to their own hearts, souls and feeling centers, because they feel the pain that this causes. And they don't need to continually stir up conflict, aggression and dissonance in order to feel empowered, or else endlessly seek greater influence, money, fame and extravagance in order to find some sense of fulfillment, when they are fulfilled within themselves by a true connection to the divine web of life.

The answer to this enduring discord that has embedded itself in the hearts of many men and plagued humanity for eons, lies in the love, wisdom and power of women. Because, coinciding with this tendency towards aggression and dominance of the stronger over the weaker within our societies, has also been a denial and subjugation of the feminine principle. It is not the feminine nature to war, to battle, to fight, to seek to destroy that which is perceived as the enemy, to resolve differences through confrontation, to seek lives of excess while the poor and the planet as a whole suffer under a way of living that's severely out of balance with the natural order.

There is more than enough of everything humans need on our abundant planet to go around, especially given remarkable advancements in modern technology that have revealed vast alternative sources of energy. For example, water-powered vehicles were on the verge of production twenty years ago, which could have completely transformed the foundations of our societies, including geopolitical changes that might have altered the course of recent wars. But this technology and many others have been repressed by the oil companies. As such, unrelenting greed on the part of some, fueled by a lack of internal fulfillment somewhere deep in their souls, keeps Earth's resources continually skewed in favor of a few insatiable elite, while billions around the world struggle to eke out a meager existence. Another good example: the recent economic crisis precipitated by a relatively small number of money-hungry individuals, mostly men, in the banking and mortgage industries in the United States, that ultimately threatened the entire world economy, and still leaves many millions unemployed and destitute, years later.

Of course, women are subject to all the frailties and imperfections mentioned here, and a long list could be made of women throughout history who have abused power and manipulated others. The point isn't that men are all to blame and women are exempt from any responsibility for humanity's and the planet's incessant problems. But it is the overarching masculine paradigm that has held sway throughout recorded human history—ignorant and blind for the most part to the complexity, sensitivity and deep-rooted power of the Divine Feminine nature—that has brought our world to where it stands today, at the brink of collapse on multiple levels. And it is when men begin awakening to some aspect of the feminine principle both within and without, and sincerely listening to, honoring and aligning with their women and with the wise, ecstatic, loving Goddess that resides within each woman, that the world will finally change in some fundamental way, and not until then.

Chapter 2

The Game of Love

What men need to understand first and foremost is that women are, for the most part, ready and in fact intensely longing for a deeply loving, dynamic relationship with men. And they've been yearning for this for a very long time. It takes two to tango as they say. But while women have been ready to dance, throwing out hints and sending alluring looks left and right, men have been lost in a game of poker, oblivious to the deeper nature of women, more transfixed by the thrilling prospects of winning or losing their life savings than exploring the true potential that lies within the dreams, feelings and longings of women.

Because in the typical unbalanced male point of view, life and love are games to be won or lost. Women are to be conquered, along with everything else they either desire or feel threatened by. Think of Tiger Woods and his mistresses, which apparently numbered more than a hundred. Being the greatest golfer in the world wasn't enough. Being rich and famous wasn't enough. Having a beautiful wife and a child wasn't enough. Even having an affair didn't satisfy him. So he had another, and another, and another, to absurdly self-indulgent extremes.

This exemplifies the big distraction that keeps many men from going deeper into themselves. There's always something more waiting somewhere just beyond reach. If they make a million dollars, then they want a million more. If they win the horse race, then they spend all the winnings hoping to win even bigger. If they win the game, the business deal, the war, the woman, then it's on to the next battle to be fought, to prove they're even more of a force to be reckoned with. And if they lose then they are no longer men, until they can regain their pride and their manhood by somehow getting back on top.

Men have been ever searching for something that remains just beyond their grasp. It's the buried treasure, the Holy Grail, the Fountain of Youth, El Dorado, Shangri-La: that something that will meet all of their expectations and desires and make them finally and truly happy and content and at peace in the world. But El Dorado, or some version of it, never existed, or was never found or else was nothing like the vision conceived of it once they got there. What men have failed to realize in the endless quest for something precious yet elusive out there in the world, is that the Holy Grail and the Fountain of Youth were both simply metaphors for something far more valuable than any material thing, which actually lies within.

At the center of this constant hunger for some hidden treasure buried at the bottom of the ocean or deep in a cave guarded by menacing dragons, is a disconnection with some long lost part of themselves. That something is feeling. That something is love. Women know this because they are the embodiment of love, feeling and emotion. They've felt the disconnect all along, and they know that the solution needed is quite plainly and simply a deeper connection between men and women on a heart and soul level. And they know that it requires men contacting some spark of the feminine within, in order to then be able to make that heartfelt connection with women.

But the masculine psyche doesn't tend to feel the disconnect, because it is mostly disconnected from feeling itself. And yet, still…something seems to be missing. There's a restlessness that keeps men wanting something more, something else, something greater. And so they continue on their quest for that tantalizing vision of some treasure out there in the world around them, searching everywhere but where it actually lies, hidden in the deepest recesses of their own consciousness. And the women, ready to dance, to engage, to make some real love, to explore the depths of human passion and potential, sit idly by, twiddling their thumbs, busying themselves with assorted tasks that help pass the time, feeling the void gnawing within them as they wait for the endless game to end.

The man folds, slams down his lousy hand of cards, goes to take a piss, grabs another beer and then heads back to the dim light of the silent table of brooding, sullen men, hoping this time he'll win big. The woman finishes the dishes, wipes her hands, glances in his direction; and knows in her heart that he's still a long ways away.

Maybe they have sex later that night. But it's just a chance for him to relieve some tension after his frustrating losses, before he turns the other way and soon enough is snoring away loudly. They may have screwed and stoked up some momentary passion. But he never actually touched her in the slightest, not the truth of who she is.

This scenario is an oversimplification of male-female relations of course, and may seem like an exaggerated one—especially to those men who have experienced fairly healthy relationships with the women in their lives. But in reality, it's probably somewhere around average. There are certainly countless examples of loving, cooperative, balanced relationships between men and women all around the world. And yet, there are also many, many abusive ones, as we all know from the news stories and statistics. But you don't hear too often about the woman who beat up her husband, because it's almost always the other way around.

It's hardly debatable that men have a much greater record of violence and mistreatment against women than vice versa, both in modern times and throughout human history. From the burning of witches to designating women as property, not allowing women to vote, keeping them veiled and hidden away in the home, not allowing them to divorce an abusive husband or even to drive a car in some countries today, to laws stating that forcible sex by a man of his wife isn't rape, or that women can't associate with men outside of their immediate family, human society is riddled with instances of male discrimination, domination and much worse against women. And yet it's hard to think of a single account of an organized campaign of prejudice by women against men. If you search hard enough through the history books then perhaps you'll find one buried away somewhere. But it will take some serious digging.

Now, in saying all this, the point isn't to engage in male-bashing and induce a guilt trip in men. That isn't at all what this book is about. The point is simply that what men need to understand and acknowledge and accept, before anything can truly change, is that women have every reason to distrust men. This is an essential realization when it comes to moving forward into a new and completely different mode of relating between the sexes. Women need to sense and feel that men have acknowledged and taken responsibility for their past mistakes, before they can trust them to move into that deeper level of relating, the one that they've been yearning and waiting for.

And this is also important to realize because this distrust and wariness has kept women hiding much of themselves from men, so that they are mere shadows of who and what they can truly be. Women have within them infinite reservoirs of radiant, creative, wise, passionate, ecstatic, orgasmic, loving energy, just waiting to be awakened, explored, honored and reveled in. And they desire a man's sensitive, attuned touch and attention and love to bring that part of themselves fully alive (or else another woman's, as the case may be). Because bringing this vibrant, pulsating, juicy energy to life requires interaction, uniting, a relationship with another.

And yet in a sense, ironically, sadly, this is precisely what keeps men away from the deeper core of women. Because on some subconscious level, men sense that women are a Pandora's Box of swirling, unfamiliar energy that they aren't quite sure they want to open up and let loose. Whatever is inside there, it seems highly volatile and unpredictable, to say the least. Better to keep a lid on it all, keep things under control and not take any chances. And besides, there's a poker game to play.

Chapter 3

Man vs. Wild

Women are indeed, to some extent, volatile and unpredictable. Deep down they are wild, untamed creatures prone to random emotions, spontaneous expression, powerful desires, unbridled passion, ever-changing moods, animalistic instincts, intuitive, irrational knowings and much more. And that is the beauty of them, to be intensely celebrated.

Men and women alike have some element of primal, unbridled essence and urgings buried deep within our brains and in our souls; which expresses itself in countless different ways, as a myriad assortment of thoughts, feelings, emotions, passions, desires, urges, aggressions, and also as basic human love. But most will probably agree that in general, men tend to tilt towards the rational, reasoned, thinking mode of being; whereas women tend to be more intuitive, feeling and emotion conscious. That's not to say that women don't have the thinking and reasoning part nailed as well, as they have proven over the past several decades in universities and in every profession that they can handle all the subjects and careers that men had previously dominated.

But there's something about emotional energy that is deemed more primal, more raw, more spontaneous and uncontrolled than the realm of thoughts and ideas. And at the center of womanhood is this wild, emotional presence, something intangible, untestable, mystifying; an energy expressed, for example, in the swaying, undulating movements of a belly-dancer, that mesmerizes and captures the attention of men and women alike. It's that expression of freely-flowing energy in motion, in a rhythm that's both hypnotically in sync, and yet at some level unpredictable and ever-changing. It is expression free of the limiting constraints of the rational mind, moving spontaneously and un-self-consciously, fully in the moment.

Emotions and feelings just want to be allowed to be free and express themselves in such a way, dancing to the music with abandon. But the rational mind lives in a different realm and tends to feel overwhelmed by the raw power of emotion. So it seeks to control it. This is, in a nutshell, the ongoing conflict between men and women.

And yet, there is obviously something in femininity that men want. Men sense that this vibrant, powerful, free-flowing energy is important and vital to life, and that it makes things interesting and life worth living. Because without women there would be no love, and without love, at least some trickle of it, there is really no point to life. So men want to be near it, want to sense it, want to dip a toe in and taste the essence of the feminine—just without having to commit to the whole enchilada. Men want to get close to women to varying degrees—just not too close, to the point where they feel as if they've lost control of things.

Women, on the other hand, want to be a heck of a lot closer. They want to merge at the heart-soul level. They want to feel that sense of oneness that they know is the real purpose of life. Because they know instinctively that the feeling of oneness with another person has the potential to inspire oneness with the whole universe; and that this feeling is our true nature and eclipses anything else as being remotely important.

To the vast majority of men, however, this sort of airy-fairy, idealistic spiritual talk, in its many forms, makes absolutely no sense. They just want to get naked and screw on a fairly regular basis, and then get a good night's sleep and get to work on time. The world of all these weird, subtle feelings, intense emotions, vague impressions and visions of something much grander happening in their relationship is a fantasy land that they don't have time or energy for, or hardly any interest in. It's the wrong direction. Men are focused on the real world around them. But women always seem to want to talk about something inside them that they just can't let go of, despite men's not-so-subtle hints that they don't really give much of a hoot.

From the man's point of view, it's the women who are never satisfied. They want more communication, more information, greater insight into the depths of your soul. They always want to know what you're thinking and feeling...when men would rather keep most of their thoughts to themselves. And if they're feeling anything at all, it's almost certainly irrelevant to the problem at hand. Either way, it's the last thing in the world they feel like talking about. Where, exactly, is the fun in that?

Why can't women just enjoy a good roll in the hay, and consider it an exclamation point at the end of a perfectly good day, rather than a question mark that requires an answer, more talking, more explanation, more discussion, more cuddling and sharing, more intimacy...something more that women are always nagging you for, when you're tired and pretty well satisfied with things at that point, and have nothing left you need to do or say?

For men, that momentary coming together in nakedness is the conclusion at the end of the book; whereas for women, it's just the end of the first chapter—and they're ready to turn the next page. They've just begun the journey of togetherness, not concluded it. But the man has the penis, and when it's spent then his mission is done and there's nothing much he can do anymore anyway...or so he thinks. And so he has a good excuse to turn the other way and call it a night. And the woman is left wanting much more.

Chapter 4

Yin and Yang

When it comes to sex, the basic reality is that the man is in the driver's seat much of the time, and the woman is hoping and yearning for him take her somewhere she actually wants to go. This is to some extent a simple matter of our different, opposite and perfectly matching sexual physiology: the penis (lingam in Indian Sanskrit, the language of the Kama Sutra, the ancient book of love) and vagina (yoni in Sanskrit). In most of the conceivable sexual positions that men and women can contort themselves into, it's necessary for the man to assume the active role, moving his lingam within her yoni, while she receives and responds to his active, masculine energy.

This simple anatomical construct automatically sets up a paradigm in which the man is in a certain amount of control over where things go. The man determines the speed, the pace, the rhythm, the force of the lovemaking, as the woman responds physically, mentally and emotionally to match the rhythm and pace set by the man. Ideally, of course, there is awareness of each other and communication, and the man also adjusts himself to accommodate the woman—as well as allows her to take the reins when she chooses, since there are plenty of options for the woman to be on top, assuming the active role herself. But otherwise, the male energy tends to be dominant.

And of course, this physical reality of the complementary opposites of male and female goes well beyond the act of sex, as it is a perfect representation of the underlying energetic distinction between masculine and feminine energies in a non-physical sense. The masculine or *yang* principle is action, force, moving forward, goal-oriented, the giver, the call. The feminine or *yin* principle is receptivity, surrender, trust, embracing, being in the moment, process-oriented, the response.

But a crucial concept to understand when it comes to finding balance between men and women—often stated but which always bears repeating—is that men are not all masculine and yang, and women are not all feminine and yin. We are each a mix of both, to wildly varying degrees. Men have some element of the feminine principle within them, as women also contain masculine energy. Some women clearly have more yang than some men, and vice versa.

Recall the Taoist yin-yang symbol in which two complementary fish-like images, one black and one white, are swirling around one another. And remember that there is a spot of black within the white symbol, and a spot of white within the black. This perfectly captures the dance of masculine (light, in this case) and feminine (dark) and is an essential piece of the puzzle. Because it embodies the fact that men and women are actually part of one unified, coexisting force of energy—not two completely separate and opposed entities. We are very different in many ways, but wholly equal and both completely necessary for one another's existence. And we are inevitably, perpetually, hopelessly intertwined with each other, now and for the rest of eternity. That's even longer than marriage. It's worth taking the time and effort to make it an enjoyable relationship.

And yet, as much as we might agree that we are all a mix of yin and yang, masculine and feminine, light and dark, that isn't to say that finding balance between men and women means throwing away all notions of gender roles and distinctions and acting like we're all the same. Because men and women are different beings, living in very different realms. As long as men are men and women are women, as long as there is the lingam and the yoni, as long as we have these human physical bodies that are so distinctly opposite, yet both necessary for the continuation of life, then men will tend towards the active, initiating role and women will tend towards the receptive and responsive. This is something we must simply acknowledge and work with. And that is the great challenge for us all in our relationships, to find the proper balance within this framework.

Now, if as a man you feel a hint of pride or superiority for being in the active, initiating position versus the feminine, then this is a good time to notice that, and hopefully get beyond it. Unfortunately, that pride on the part of men for having the penis, and everything that goes along with it, has been the source of countless problems between men and women throughout the ages.

If there's any truth to the concept of penis envy on the part of women, then underneath it most likely is penis resentment, and for good reason. Men have used and abused the potent power of their penises, both literally and figuratively, in every way they can possibly get away with it, to the detriment of the more subtle and less, well, cocky powers of the feminine. Men are continually obsessed with proving the largeness and greatness of their manhood, both destructively and creatively, and often simply for the sake of it—as evidenced by countless phallic symbols erected around the world such as the Eiffel Tower and the Space Needle, which are of little real use to anyone other than to provide a view and, more importantly, to state boldly to all who witness it: "Here I am, a man who designed and accomplished something."

But simply having a cock isn't something to get too puffed up in pride about. Roughly half the world has one, more than three billion people. And, believe it or not, you didn't actually create it. God did (or the processes of evolution, if you prefer) and handed out one of the only two available options somewhat willy-nilly: penis, vagina, penis, vagina, penis, vagina. Sure, have pride in your manhood, just as women should have pride in their womanhood. For both sexual organs are beautiful things that are capable of great pleasure, not to mention necessary for human life. However, that is a different sort of pride than one of superiority for simply being male.

Instead of pride for representing the masculine side of the equation, there's something else that men should feel: responsibility. Because along with power comes accountability (which, of course, applies equally to the powers of the feminine). But due to the underlying nature of our sexual as well as energetic differences, plus the cultural customs that have grown out of these distinctions, men have a great deal of affect on the overall state of relationships between men and women. In short, a woman's happiness is to a significant extent hinged on your ability as a man to love her. Of course, it goes both ways. But as stated previously, women are already open to being loved and to loving. They are waiting for men to reciprocate. This means that it's the man's decision—to turn towards the woman or else to turn away—that will really make all the difference.

As a result of all these complex dynamics of male and female, yin and yang existing on multiple levels, and epitomized by that basic act of the masculine lingam entering and being received and embraced by the feminine yoni, a woman's pleasure, satisfaction, joy and happiness is to some extent in a man's hands. The man is the movement, and the woman is the experience of and response to that movement. So be aware and conscious of how you move within women, physically and in all other ways, because that movement has the power to bring great pleasure, as well as to bring pain. And when men choose to ignore the effects of how they relate to women, then everyone loses. But women feel the effects the most.

And correspondingly, all of the beautiful, loving, orgasmic feminine energy that resides within each woman is available to men to experience, to the extent that they are attuned to the feminine, seek out its vulnerable essence and are willing to enter some unknown territory in the process. Women have been waiting a long time for men to give up all the silly games of distraction and get down to loving them deeply and profoundly.

When they do, men will discover that there is another world, another dimension to life right under their noses, that they have been completely overlooking their entire lives while searching for something else.

Women pretty much know what they want, even if with all their attempts at communication they don't get around to telling you directly. Women want to connect, interact, engage, share, learn, live, love and grow with men in a mutually cooperative and respectful partnership. Men, on the other hand, aren't so sure they want to take it to that level. Because it takes them into a realm of mystery and the unknown, the darkness within.

There is a depth to women and feminine energy that most men are simply nowhere near seeing, not to mention understanding. This book is about bridging that divide between men and women, by giving men some useful information and tools to allow them to better understand a woman's point of view—and, deeper still, a woman's heart. But it requires a concerted persistence on the part of the man to find that place within a woman because, simply put, women are complicated. And they've been let down and disregarded too often to truly open up to a man when he finally opens his eyes a little wider and takes a deeper look. Women need to know that you aren't just going to stick a toe in, so to speak, and then decide not to take a swim. Women want to know that you're going to stick around for the next round, and take it to the next level. Because that's when the real dance, the real lovemaking begins.

Chapter 5

Undressing the Goddess

There are many different levels and layers to the minds, hearts and souls of women, which can be peeled away and removed as are layers of clothing, leaving them even more naked and exposed than the physical form could ever be. At their core women are deeply sensitive, vulnerable, wide open, profoundly loving and also powerful, intense beings. But don't expect to discover the most deep-rooted, primal nature of a woman right away, or necessarily in this lifetime.

Penetrating and merging with these different layers of a woman requires corresponding levels of trust and commitment. Even women themselves aren't necessarily aware of these different dimensions within themselves, certainly not fully.

Of course everyone, men and women alike, has multiple levels and aspects to who they are, based on the millions of things we've experienced in our lifetimes, positive and negative, consequential and seemingly insignificant, that have made us the complex beings we are. But women on the whole tend to be closer to that deeper nature of loving potential within us all. And they are also hungering to a greater extent to reconnect with that potential within us, and to take human relations to the next level of intimacy, and then to the next one after that.

The most important thing is to simply have the intention that you want to experience a more meaningful, loving, honest and more dynamic relationship with your woman, or with women in general. Don't think that you can just go up to your girlfriend or wife or lover and say, "Honey, I've been reading this book that's changed my mind about some things, and now everything is going to be different between us"...and expect that everything is, in fact, going to be different between the two of you. Old habits and patterns die hard. Men say they're going to change all the time...and then they don't. Women pretty much expect to be let down and disappointed by the lofty aspirations of men in the relationship department.

Start small, and see where it leads. It's much more important to work at the subconscious levels, than at the conscious levels. Allow your simple intention to guide you in seeking and finding a new level of relating, and of being more fully present in your relationship and in yourself. Women will, in some part of themselves, pick up on the fact that you've made a basic shift of intention...that you've opened your eyes a little wider to see who they really are. And most likely (though not necessarily right away), they will open themselves up a little more to meet you, as you make the conscious choice to get closer to them.

Feel things out and take your time. Be prepared to meet roadblocks, be thrown backwards, meet unpleasant emotions or circumstances, lose your way and make mistakes. It will be a learning experience for both of you to make a commitment to finding a deeper experience of love, pleasure and ultimately ecstasy, since most people have barely scratched the surface, men or women.

This process means more than simply going to a new place. It also requires changing who you are along the way. If a woman is going to truly open up to a man, she needs to know and trust that he actually wants to be there, that he's ready to go the distance, and that he can handle being and staying present with her as she opens up and exposes more of herself.

And along with that intention to change your relationship, you'll need to make another commitment. That is to allow yourself to learn something from your woman—and not just something, but a lot. That doesn't mean that everything she says is right, and everything you know to be true is wrong. It means committing to a mutually beneficial relationship of learning from and evolving along with one another. It means seeing your relationship as a journey of adventure and discovery, and choosing to see your woman as a source of great knowledge and wisdom.

If you're not really that interested in taking a deeper look at yourself, but just want women to be more interesting and attractive to you, then you might as well just put this book down. If you're not ready to actually make a change at your own core being to some extent, then any changes in the right direction will only be on the very surface and won't amount to much in the long run. You've got to be ready to open not only your eyes but your ears, and hear what your woman has to say...as well as what she's really saying underneath what she's saying. In short, you've got to listen—and not just with your ears and your mind, but with your heart and with your soul.

Chapter 6

Stop and ask for directions

Whether or not, as the man, you happen to find yourself in the driver's seat, there's something important to keep in mind: *the woman has the map*. The age-old scenario is that the man is so attached to acting like he's in charge and knows where he's going, that he would rather drive around in circles, hoping to stumble across his destination by chance, than stop and ask someone to help him out and tell him how to get there.

But if you're finally tired of endlessly driving around in circles in your relationship, and ready to humble yourself a bit and admit that you could make use of some clues, then look no further than your own woman. Women tend to know intuitively when the relationship is going in the right direction and when it isn't. This is to a great extent because relationships are in the realm of the invisible. And women more often have a greater knack in this department than men.

Relationships are all about the unseen. A relationship isn't something easily defined or grasped, that you can say definitively: "Here it is, this is what it looks like, where it is and what it consists of". They are primarily about feelings, emotions, impressions, thoughts, ideas, assumptions, agreements, visions, desires, exchanges and connections on subtle, subconscious planes of being.

Men generally prefer to deal with things they can get their hands on and manipulate through force. We love the exhilaration that comes from resolving a good challenge such as a car that's stuck in the snow, or a lug nut that won't come off, or a game that must be won. The problems that come up in relationships are a different story, however, and can't be solved through the same sorts of brute tactics in the slightest. They involve experiences and exchanges going on within and between people that can be hard to be aware of even at the time, let alone deal with and straighten out sometime after the fact; such as when your woman comes to you distressed about some offhand remark you made that you don't even remember. This is why women are always wanting more communication. Because they are more in touch with the unseen realms, and they want to be there in the present moment, to look at what's really going, know what each other is REALLY thinking and feeling, explore it, be aware of those subtle things under the surface, deal with them and make sense of them.

And one of the reasons for this is because there's this deeper level of relating that women want to engage in, this other realm of deeply loving interaction that most relationships are pretty much disconnected from. There's another world that women want to enter into with men and explore together. And they have the map to it because they know subconsciously, in the very essence of their being that there is a much deeper love available to everyone to be experienced, if they could just guide men into that place, or else be guided there—whatever it takes to make it happen.

But as long as men are insistent on being the ones in charge, unwilling to consider the real input of women as they drive around in circles, acting like they know where they're going and as if they don't need any more information, then there remains this gap, and in many cases a chasm, between men and women that can seem impossible to bridge.

Chapter 7

Attuning to the feminine

If you really want to discover the true potential that exists between men and women, and begin to experience the depths of intensely loving, orgasmic, ecstatic energy that resides within the hidden layers of women, then the most important thing, at first, is just to make that commitment to learn something from the wisdom of the feminine. Accept the idea that women have within them vital keys to life; that they hold within them that map to a hidden treasure, in another world in which life is more colorful and interesting and love and pleasure is more abundant.

With that in mind, open your eyes and ears a bit wider. Be willing to listen more, acknowledge more, see deeper into the realms of the feminine, and recognize that your woman has a voice and ideas that are wholly equal to your own. Who knows, they might even be better a lot of the time. Be willing to be wrong, and let whoever has the right answer bring you both to a better place of being, a more enjoyable experience of life and love. Make the intention to create a relationship where the energy flows back and forth between you, so that you are both giving and both receiving from each other, and learning about each other in the process—rather than sticking to your positions that you're right and that's all there is to it.

Again, that isn't to say that in an idyllic world men and women should blur the lines, drop everything that defines them and stop being distinctly male or female, masculine or feminine. Masculinity is a beautiful thing; femininity is a beautiful thing. They are very different energies and represent starkly different modes of being. Finding balance between the sexes doesn't have to mean, for example, that you make sure the woman is on top exactly 50% of the time, in the bedroom or otherwise. The important thing is simply for men and women to both be happy with the arrangement, whatever it is, rather than women putting up with things as they are and accepting that it's just how things have to be whether they like it or not, or vice versa. What needs to happen is simply for men and women to open up to one another more, and engage in a mutually accommodating relationship in which they are both learning about each other's differing points of view, and thus evolving and growing towards one another. That's the way to bridge the gap.

But the thing is, women are accustomed already to opening to men. Women have always heard the voices of men. The thoughts and ideas and desires and visions of men are everywhere and have always been out there in the open for everyone to see and consider. It's the voices of women which have been stifled and ignored, hidden away in the dark, suppressed, distorted and ridiculed. And as a result their wisdom, their perspective and input that could bring balance and thus real peace, harmony and love to life and to the world, has been missing.

So the burden is really on the men now to realize that, although our male-dominated societies throughout recent history have produced wondrous, great things, whether it's grand buildings and sprawling cities, high-tech lasers and modern medicine, airplanes and computers, advanced weaponry, space technology, cell phones, the internet and the list could go on ad infinitum, something important is still missing. Something is out of balance. For all the important developments that have been made in recent decades in the equalizing of the sexes, we still have a ways to go, especially in certain parts of the world.

I won't bore you with a long account of all the signs that our planet is in a state of crisis, as we see the evidence all around us now, becoming more and more difficult to ignore and deny. And ultimately it isn't something that can be proven. It can only be sensed, felt, intuitively known that things aren't quite as they should be in the world and within humanity today, and that a big part of the solution is that the Goddess, the feminine principle, the wisdom of women is being ignored, and must now awaken and rise to take her rightful place as an equal alongside the male God who has hovered over our cultures without a balancing counterpart.

So I hope that you will enjoy, as well as gain some useful information from what some very intelligent and creative women—manifestations of the Divine Feminine nature—have to say about all of these thought-provoking topics in Part 2 of this book. And then, you'll hear some more intriguing perspectives from the masculine side of things, in Part 3.

Part 2:

Women Speak

Cosmic Union

By Tracy Cooper

Are you a God wielding lightning with your hand, a heroic champion on a truth quest, a warrior ferociously steeled, silently stalking your next meal, a romantic creatively weaving words of homage to your lover, a gregarious lion ready to pounce, or an adventurer waiting for life to call? At different times, you have inhabited the souls of all these great men. A new role is calling. Can you hear the rustle in the wind, in your breath as you exhale, the buzzing in your ears beginning as a low hum and gaining momentum to the fever pitch heard by astronauts hitting the sound barrier, rattling the depths, forcing you to action?

You are not alone.

Destiny is inviting women at this time in history to shake off old outworn clothes and beliefs and step into the Sun, taking our rightful place again as Goddesses of the Earth. Do you feel the women around you changing, growing, throwing off perceived shackles and bindings, coming into their own, a light switch lighting up a semi-darkened room?

Yet, we need you. All women need a hero, a prince, a king to stand beside and shine with us—God and Goddess. Do you feel it, men? The philosophical question: is will you remain in a stagnant pool, or will you shake off traditional roles, be fluid and playful? Can you stand as a man confidently while simultaneously allowing the sun to shine beside you? Can you balance being supportive without being submissive? Can you pursue your own divine path while encouraging ours?

The 21st century summons men and women to create a cosmic union, an alchemical marriage. We need a partner, husband, lover, father and conspirator-in-love to celebrate life together.

For centuries, crusades spanned continents to achieve power, dominate and colonize the world. Based on our technological advances, our experience today is extraordinary and complicated; yet, with the recent local and foreign impacts from economic fraud, overconsumption and greed, there is a new movement gaining ground towards life simplification involving universal love and truth.

There have always been expeditions in search of some mystical, elusive Holy Grail just out of man's reach. What if all along we have been in search of a singular truth? Lying deep within us is a knowing, and it is our time to decide: shall we choose unity and allow our roles to evolve with the tuning fork of universal harmony?

As creators of our new world, how do we manifest our visions of positive relations between the sexes? The cyclical nature of time allows us to benefit from and recreate new storyboards from history. Archeological research depicts the Neolithic period as demonstrating no signs of warfare, a time where the Great Goddess reigned in a complimentary nature with men in society, allowing for prosperity, peace, collaboration and community. Similarly today, the Nordic region has a strong tradition of men and women working together, and research from the United Nations demonstrates the collaboration is beneficial, naming Norway the best place in the world to live for the last six years.

Men and women everywhere are ready for change in order to live a better, more balanced, more purposeful life. The only option is to live on purpose!

The Goddess is crawling out of the darkness, emerging with a holiness of self, waiting to be released. For centuries, women's primary focus was ensuring the happiness of everyone around her, leaving the nurturing of her own soul to the ethers. Women are no longer willing to smile through the resentment, and are beginning to see the truth of being whole and loving ourselves fiercely.

We need you, truly we do need you. With the expertise of a pelican dive-bombing deep into the sea, will you meet us as two porpoises gliding fluidly, playing through the waves in the space between? The 21st century adventurer diverges from an emphasis on individual pursuits, to focused intention for the greater good of the collective.

What can be better for all than the joining of Adam and Eve, Sun and Moon, God and Goddess?

Step away from the destructive ledge of self-pity, depreciation, guilt and a voracity for satiation. Rather, keep it simple and make the time for unabashed truth and unconditional love.

Everything else is just water trying to fill up a cracked jar.

Have you forgotten what it means to love unconditionally? It's easy…I always imagine myself in Yosemite where, hidden under a bridge lies a massive rock outcropping and a splendid roaring waterfall. Join me and imagine yourself deep in the woods, standing in front of your waterfall, a Waterfall of Love. You step in with one foot…and then the other, immersing yourself into the chilly waters and quickly, while you have your courage, dive just under the surface and effortlessly reach down deep into the clear waters, feeling your body being filled with light and love, down to the cellular level. Open your eyes and swim directly under the waterfall, lifting your face, allowing the refreshing Adam's ale, shimmering with reflections of sunlight, to splash down on your face and head, releasing the tension in your shoulders and providing peace, love and light to your mind and heart.

This purity, this essence is the feeling to expand to others in everything you do. Will you meet me in the light, and together, let us create a rich, full life?

Truly the most beloved lesson one can live is to bring their loving spirit to every moment, remove all duality and confusion and know simply there is only love and light within you and around you. Choose to shine your truth brightly to everyone, and remember only one thing, LOVE. Open your heart to everyone and everything and love truly, deeply, unconditionally, and your life and those you touch will be a blessing beyond measure.

May you enjoy the beautiful journey!

Tracy Uloma Cooper, Ph.D., hails from the Bay Area, and was raised under the teachings of Unity and A Course in Miracles. Previously a counselor with UC Berkeley's Psychological Services department, Tracy's heightened psychological healing as a metaphysician works at the anatomy of a spirit level. Recognizing what makes people really tick and moving to the cause, the true cause, of their imbalances and their weariness with the world…empowering individuals to awaken and author one's own passionate beautiful life! (For newsletter/appointments, e-mail: Tracycoopr@yahoo.com or find her on Facebook: Tracy Cooper ~ The Rose Line)

The Truth Within a Woman

By Anaya Thomas

A woman is a mother, a sister, a wife, a daughter. Go deeper, and you will find she has many different titles, responsibilities and duties to attend to. As women we struggle, and in so doing we find ourselves filled with emotions from so many different areas of our hearts.

The journey starts with the birth of innocence, then takes us through love, heartbreaks, tears of joy, sometimes of sadness or even anger, because we were hurt. The insecurities within ourselves might manifest from the way that society views what a "real woman" is so often expected to look like. Must a real woman be one who has a tight tummy, firm buttocks, big breasts, full lips? Must she be a woman drawn in the image of perfection inside a man's mind?

A real woman is a Goddess of expression and a manifestation of the true Divine Mother. We are naturally made perfect the way we are, and the way we were supposed to be. We are divine spirits who carry life continuously, lifetime after lifetime. We give birth to man and woman; we breathe life into a new life. A real woman is nurturing, compassionate, loving and understanding. She sometimes carries more then she can handle, and manages to find the strength inside herself to carry on. She's a fighter for what she believes in, yet she walks with grace. She is often expected to be only that limited vision that a man desires her to be. Yet she yearns to be loved for who she truly is; not for who anyone else wants her to be. When you drop that expectation of being something else, then she becomes real in your eyes. She wants to be acknowledged not just for her body, but for her heart: that which seeks the love of a King, a Nobleman, a Warrior. Her beautiful glowing spirit lights the path for many. See beyond the physical beauty of her body, because she contains within her more than mere physical pleasure. Her heart is a soft lotus, a flower of color and of life. A woman is seeking a greater depth of loving awareness within herself and within her lover.

To love and honor a woman is to acknowledge her with grace, with a humility that is both firm and proud. Feel her within your heart, breathe deep, take the beauty of her light and inhale it into you. See beyond your mind, which has been programmed to see a woman as only a human body to quench your thirst. Connect with your own heart. A woman is a child of the divine essence. She stands as a Goddess before you who is worth more than only a vision of your ecstasy. She is a fragile flower, yearning to be watered with your unconditional masculine divine love. She is the connection from one divine mother to the next divine woman; powerful in pleasure, passionate in her true existence of this universe.

When she expresses her feelings, just listen. When she seeks to feel your love, share your heart with passion. When she cries, just embrace her tight. When she is happy, celebrate that happiness with her. When she looks at you and smiles, it's a reminder of the beauty of love that you both share. A woman communicates in many different ways, sometimes verbally, sometimes mentally, in writing, through emotions and at times even in silence. This communication can begin with a simple thought that is provoked, which moves into our hearts and then transforms into an emotion, as we set it free by expressing it to you. That emotion is desire; it is love. Allow it to flow forth and connect man and woman as one.

A woman desires to be honored, not suppressed, and carried into the light of divine love. As women, we realize that sometimes it's not easy to understand us. But we are an energy that is the balancing force in this paradigm...moving towards a oneness with the Divine Masculine. Honor the Goddess in the highest form of love, and in return she will honor you.

Anaya Thomas is a Certified Kids Yoga Instructor, C.M.T, Wedding Coordinator and on a strong mission to empower and bring back the Goddess Energy. She is also the creator of The Primal Feminine, a spiritual group and network of Divine Women and Men that seeks to bring forth the Goddess Movement. Her desire to rebirth the true meaning of rights and freedom as a woman has contributed in helping to heal the imbalance between men and women. Her future goals will include beautiful exotic journeys and ecstatic dances that embrace both feminine and masculine essence in the true honoring of themselves and each other. Please contact her for further details. Facebook: The Primal Feminine, Website: www.meetup.com/The-Primal-Feminine-and-Masculine/ Email: primalfeminine@hotmail.com or info@wigglesngig-glesyoga.com

I Want Burning: Loving a Woman on the Spiritual Path

By Kylie Devi

As I see it, there are two types of relationships people have with each other. There is the need-based, emotionally attached, I'll-do-this-if-you-do-that type of being with each other; or there is a relationship where two people (or perhaps more) choose from a space of love, freedom and awareness, cultivating interactions from an evolved perspective.

In the second type of relationship, participants must let go of attachment, expectation and projections. However, boundaries are perfectly acceptable. It is not an "anything goes free-for-all" just because it is a relationship based on the principles of spiritual freedom. Rather, the foundation of this type of relating is integrity, trust and a profound sense of respect for the other as self. We do not intentionally play games, inflict harm or attempt to deceive in this platform. We gently nudge the other when they fall prey to illusory mental phenomena that cause suffering, and we always remember that even if we do become seduced by this type of trickery, that the other is never the cause of our suffering and we are responsible for what we perceive and how we act based on our perception. There is no exception to this, and we are impeccable with it.

I must say that loving a woman—and loving a woman well—is one of the finer accomplishments a man or woman could achieve in this lifetime. Loving her spirit and allowing her to be totally free is a gorgeous offering to this planet. Women, like the Earth herself, have been subjugated, dominated and controlled for somewhere around 6,000 years now; so loving a woman wholly while allowing her to express herself fully is almost a revolutionary contribution to human development and the evolution of consciousness. The constraining social and cultural paradigms we have lived in for the last several millennia has been, for women, like a flower that is allowed to grow at the stem alone, the beautiful petals being plucked before they are ready, exploited, rushed…and then sent into a torrent of wind, landing here and there but never really shining with the depth of beauty that her essence was born to be.

There are feminists and scholars who explain this phenomenon, and there is also a trace of anger in some schools of thinking about the whole thing. I am not here to man bash or purport any type of hatred. I am simply bringing up a historical fact that can explain much about the collective psyche of the female mind. She in fact is much more primal, more body-centered, more wild and more loving then we have allowed her to be. Let's allow her to be, then.

Have you ever loved the type of woman who simply cannot be captured? Her beauty shines through strikingly even in the most mundane of moments. And yet, you cannot quite fathom what her beauty is made of. She is wild one moment and peaceful the next; ecstatic for no comprehensible reason, and then sobbing into her hands at something you can't perceive or relate to only minutes later. In her eyes you see the depths of the universe; yet she can seem so youthful, innocent. It almost seems as if she needs your protection, but then... there she goes, she is free. She is untamable. She is likely to do the most profound things you have conceived of, and then on a whim make choices that perplex and stupefy, but which generally receive no explanation other than a coy smile. This, my Beloveds, is the story of any man or woman who has ever loved a woman who is in love with Love, the mystic fire.

Rumi writes:

"I want burning, burning;
Be friends
with your burning. Burn up your thinking
and your forms of expression!
Moses,
those who pay attention to ways of behaving
and speaking are one sort.
Lovers who burn are another."

(From "Moses and the Shepherd," by Rumi, tr. Coleman Barks)

This most certainly refers to the second type of relationship I mentioned. And if you are in love with a woman who understands this type of burning, this type of yearning for union with the Divine, then you are in for a real ride. Nothing is scripted out for you to better understand. There is no instruction manual, no how-to book that will get you any real points. No conference, convention, coaching or e-book will prepare you for this. The only rule written in stone is that you must be willing to sacrifice any part of yourself that is not real, that you have held onto for safety, comfort or social standing.

You must allow all of this to be thrown into the fire. If you have studied any Eastern religions at all, than you are familiar with the Yab-Yum (a tantric pose in which the man sits cross-legged and the woman sits on top of him, face to face and embracing one another). Male and female deities engage in a complete and loving union. We Westerners have adapted this ancient wisdom into what is now known as "neo-tantra," which is a set of practices relating to sexuality, awareness and ecstatic living. The practices range from breathing, to becoming more aware of our bodies and our desires, to making love in a spiritual or elevated consciousness.

However, the tantric masters of ancient lineages did not prescribe sexual practices to students until they had become very advanced and adept at the skill of self mastery. This is because while we are on the spiritual path, cultivating practices that accumulate power, we must have mastery over our own energy before we attempt to share it. We cannot share this energy casually. The energy must be received by those who are prepared for it.

Ancient tantric practitioners were making love to their own empty awareness. They had awakened to their deeper self, to the truth of who they really Are. And in this, they would never be able to inflict harm upon each other because this is the space from which devotional love, true love, arises.

So please only make love to a woman if you know in your heart that you will never consciously harm her or yourself. Some say the Yab-Yum stands for the merger between Compassion and Wisdom. When you are in love with a woman on the spiritual path, meet her as Compassion would meet Wisdom. Do not do this sometimes. Do it always; and she will give you more happiness than you even conceived was available through a relationship. You will know yourself as Divine, as Whole, as Completely Free. And she will love you. She will love you in ways you never thought possible.

Kylie Devi is a writer and activist who works in the healing arts field assisting others to transform trauma into radical self-acceptance, compassionate action and powerful purpose. She is currently working on two books: *Love After Rape* and *Shakti Awake: Recovering the Spirit from Sexual Trauma.* A native New Yorker, she currently lives in Gainesville, Florida and spends most of her time writing, practicing yoga and qigong, organizing art and poetry events and performing spoken word art. You can subscribe to her blog at www.kyliedevi.com or connect with her on facebook at www.facebook.com/kyliedevi.

To Be Loved By A Man

By Asttarte Deva Shakti Bliss

I know what it feels like to be loved by a man—a man whose heart is open wide to the spirit you are; a man who loves you, or in the moment feels as though he is deeply in love with you.

...To be held in his arms; to feel his breath upon your chest as he holds you in embrace and caresses your heart into deep utter relaxation.

...To be teased into bliss by the simplicity of his eyes melting into yours.

You never forget what it feels like to be held by a man—a man, not a boy or a child, and not your father or your son. A man, who is so deeply in love with YOU!

His rich smell as his pheromones reach out to yours and tantalize your adrenaline into heaven.

A spark of simplicity, a whimper in your heart of relief, of satisfaction, of knowing you are woman, as you are received in his love and accepted for being the Goddess you are!

What a gift you are receiving in being loved by his depth, in knowing you ARE Goddess and are powerful in your femininity; a divine being worthy of being loved.

What a gift he is receiving, in giving him the experience of loving you, in knowing he is capable of loving and valuable in being received.

To be loved by a man offers so many gifts, for both the receiver and the giver. To be a woman, being loved by a man helps you to know you ARE alive, and you are worthy, are capable and acceptable in being a Woman; a wise woman, an innocent woman, a powerful woman, a vulnerable woman; that you are allowed to be YOU, and you are allowed to be Goddess.

You have permission and you need not shut down your prowess, your sensuality or your love!

Some thoughts to consider:

1) As a man, what does it mean to be loved by a woman to you?
2) What does it offer you to love a woman? And, what does it mean to you to love a woman, who truly receives your love?
3) How often do you allow yourself to be truly loved by your wife/girlfriend?
4) Are you a man who doesn't like talking about feelings and wishes the problems or issues would just go away? Would you rather wish them away than deal with them? What are you afraid of that makes you want to run when it comes to feelings?
5) If you had it your way, what would you want your current relationship to look like, feel like and smell like? I.e. what would your surroundings and environment be, how would your partner behave towards you, how would they treat you, how would you treat them, where would you live, and what would you have in your home, how would you get along with in-laws and friends in social outings?
6) Are you typically the leader in your relationship and the first to bend to work out an argument, or are you the one who holds grudges and waits to see if, maybe, things will work out on their own? If you did become the leader, what would you do or say to your partner to help them open their heart to you again?
7) If you are not receiving the type of love that you really want, ask yourself, what is it that you want, and what in your relationship is missing, if you had it your way, that you would want to be there?

Why is it that men are so often sexually frustrated? I would like to elaborate on this from a woman's perspective and offer a viewpoint that you might not have considered, and perhaps give you something to contemplate for a while.

Women grow up as young girls, and often as young girls we are extremely sensitive to the things around us. We as children are more open, intuitive and feel more intensely than we do as adults. We feel like Healers do, and have higher perceptions of things around us.

Young girls often go through life having to defend themselves, fight off people who cross their boundaries where they feel threatened just for being soft, feminine and girly. These young girls are easier prey to those bigger than them and get picked on easier and sometimes, although not wanted, the worst case scenarios take place and we get raped. And, oftentimes all of these confusing and scarring things that happen to us get ignored and many times forgotten.

These girls then try to go through life as if nothing ever happened. We live, we move on and we survive. But, yet we have deep hidden pains inside of us. As young girls we aren't really aware how we were damaged. We have strong wills and like to have fun. As young women, we express our sexuality and party all the time. But as adults, as fully integrated women, it catches up with us. By this time we are married, we have children and are fully into our careers. Our husbands and boyfriends don't know about our pains and can't understand why we act the way we do at times, but we know, deeply!

Then it dawns on our husbands that they want more sex. They are frustrated. They aren't getting it, and inside of us, our hearts are broken. Women are often so suppressed that they aren't even in touch with the pain inside of them. Sometimes they are, but don't think it's possible to heal, or worse, don't want to. We need to be nurtured, loved, caressed and cared for as a Goddess and fully respected as women, in a way that includes and embracing our femininity, our vulnerability and our traumas. We need to take the time to open our hearts and expand the flower that we were meant to be. But, the husbands we are with are frustrated. They are impatient, and they want instant satisfaction. And they aren't getting it for the exact reason that their adrenaline is high and their patience becomes thin. They become demanding, needy and pushy. And as women, we see this as a turn off. We pull away. We need safety and aren't getting it. We feel threatened and unloved, and the distance between the two of us becomes larger. Eventually the split from heart and body takes place and sex becomes not something of intimacy or love, but of need and often demand.

And a lot of you men out there are wondering why your wives aren't horny! Well, we women have been through hell, and YOU need to become our Healers, or we will put up a wall from you. So, my dear gentleman, I am here to tell you and teach you, you MUST become a gentleman and give your woman the nurturing and the softer heart of yours that she first fell in love with. Otherwise, distance will prevail and overshadow any potential relationship you have.

My wish is for all men to learn to listen, to hear what the women of the world truly need and to open your hearts to love them. This then, is when the women of the world will TRULY give you ALL the love you ever wanted!

Asttarte Deva is the founder and owner of Center for Intimacy & Life Enhancement. Asttarte is a relationship coach and offers solutions in sexual issues, spiritual direction or guidance, family problems from the past or present, intimacy fears, phobias or frustrations, solutions for singles and dating, health & wellness concerns and general life problems in the way. She is also a Massage Therapist, Advanced IET Practitioner, Tera-Mei Seichem, Shamballa and Lotus Light Reiki Master, Yoga Teacher, a Certified Melchizedek Priestess, a Holistic Practitioner,

Spiritual Shamanic Healer, and Initiated Ancient Egyptian Goddess. She offers integrated Healing Retreat and Coaching Sessions combining professional coaching, meditation, holistic healing and massage therapy. She is here to express her creative passions, share love with the world and guide you on your journey! She has an ongoing blog at SexBlissLifeCoach .blogspot.com and her main business site is at: Intimacy andLifeEnhancementCenter.com. She is located outside of Philadelphia, PA and lives with her son.

How to Love a Goddess

By P. Maya Morgan

As I was growing into my age of independence of self, I explored different cultures and surrounded myself with new people, as different from how I myself had been raised, incubated by my family. I thought I was an independent girl with enough smarts, common sense, blond hair and long legs to achieve whatever I wanted in life. Yet I was insecure in my relationships with men. I gave over my power to men due to my insecurities and need to "be loved".

My history of relationships repeated a pattern of physical love, without the depth of real connection. I realized I could easily "be loved" by plenty of men. That was not the issue. I wanted to be honored and seen for my deeper self. Through my loving sisters (Goddesses) and my connection to nature, I learned that the true way to love was to first honor my sacred self. I could only nurture and love myself first and foremost. Men could not offer me that. I found my true inner light/inspiration by being alone or with my sisters. Being in nature supplied the introduction into my states of harmony with One. By caring for and honoring the Earth, I in turn honored myself. While backpacking in the wilderness, swimming in turquoise seas or breathing the crisp thin air on a snow covered mountain top, I became aware of my connection to Her power and it empowered me to view the world and my experiences in a different way. It took me down a pathway of conservation and of learning what I could from Her beauty. I sought out solitary times in nature, and listened to the messages that blew through the pines.

Goddesses are Earthkeepers who are loving and caring for our Mother Earth. The Native American Indians were natural

Earthkeepers, by only taking what they needed. I honored and sought out their wisdom through honoring my own monthly cycles, and by celebrating the turning of the seasons with my Goddess sisters. We studied and taught ourselves the values of herbal treatments, aromatherapy and yoga. Goddess brings back the Ancient Earth Wisdoms.

Women have been given the gift of compassion, the gifts of expressing emotions and feelings, and most of all, the gift to nurture. We are bringers of life, not destroyers. There is no question that men innately want to be nurtured and cared for. But it's difficult for them to reciprocate on a level that women truly appreciate. Women have learned through history to self-nurture, or surround themselves with other woman who can nurture each other.

We seek balance through honoring the Feminine. In order to evolve mankind forward, we must bring the balance back toward Feminine strength—not brute force. With more and more conscious men becoming aware of this inequality and honoring the Feminine inside themselves, then we move closer to our purpose. Men must learn to use our Feminine power to heal their hurts, and express their emotions just as little boys being held tight by their mothers. It's the perfect mother's love and the place we all want to return to—being held and told that everything will be okay, as you cry your emotions.

I recognize the power in the Feminine, and how that balance may heal the Earth. Listening to the insecurities, hurts and feelings of women while holding us tight can bring us closer to Her heart source. We don't expect men to fix our insecurities, but to hear what we are saying and acknowledge us with a deeper understanding.

My experience has been that men rarely listen in a deep, truly open or undefended way. Women have decades of suppression to release. Allowing us to open our wounds in a safe place can create trust between the two halves. This is huge, men. Trusting you completely is one of the big secrets and/or keys to our many levels of soothing and healing love. When we trust men in this world, we have a whole lot of healing/loving energy that can circulate through the consciousness of the planet. We want to sympathize with and nurture our men. Wouldn't it be great if men could have empathy with our past experiences and insecurities? I guess that's where the war between the sexes continues. Women are "emotional basket cases" and men are "stubborn defensive asses". Is it possible for the two to live in harmony? Seems like compromise by one or the other must be inevitable.

Through the power and love of the Goddess we can rekindle the flame of our spirits. In relationship with my sisters, we create a sacred safe place where we can be our true selves. Why is it so hard to feel sacred, honored and acknowledged by our men? When my sisters honor me, and ask nothing by my truth and light, it creates the space where I feel beautiful and full of light! So men, listen up: When you make us feel beautiful, safe, honored and cherished, our lights will brighten and shine all over you!

But wait, there's more! This is only one level into the Divine Feminine. Women have several gated walls that men must find the keys to, in order to open that inner sanctum of inner wisdom, true inspiration, and the peak of sexual desirability. I came across a piece written lovingly by Arjuna Ardagh, who has become an awakened man.

He states: "Open another gate with your commitment, with your attention, and with the small seedlings of devotion, and she'll open her heart to you more. She'll share with you her insecurities, the way that she's been hurt, her deepest longings. Some men will back away at this point. They realize that the price they must pay to go deeper is more than they are willing to give."

Mr. Ardagh continues with great knowledge and understanding: "For those few who step through another gate, they come to discover her loyalty. Somewhere around the second wall from the center, she casts the veils of her personality aside, and shows you that she is both a human being and also a portal into something much greater. She shows you a wrath that is not hers, but all women portrayed as Gods & Goddesses!"

Arjuna continues: "The very essence of this innermost temple is the sacred Feminine, the One divine flame. These gates are opened magically and invisibly by the keys of worship. If you make a practice of telling your woman something you adore about her daily, I guarantee she'll open to you in a way you've never seen before."

Words of adoration are like music to our ears! And the Goddess loves to dance. Since men love touch, touch her in adoring, sweet ways (no, don't just grab her ass) and she'll reciprocate in ways unimagined. It's the "small seedlings of devotion" and honoring expressions that hand you the keys to her inner temple.

P. Maya Morgan resides in the Santa Cruz Mountains, California. She is a self-exploring writer, yogini, gardener, mother, kayaker and earth worshiper of all natural beauty, including a lifelong Sierra Club activist/hiker. Many thanks to my Sisters of the Sacred Circle of Santa Cruz for inspiring me to write and for publishing various personal empowerment articles in the *Goddess Circle News*. She is currently in the process of writing stories of her solo travel adventures. P.O. Box 1407, Felton, CA 95018.

Dear Husband

By Alice Grist

It's time I talked to you about what a fabulous Goddess you really are. You truly have a dose of the Divine Feminine about you, my dear. Now, hubby, I know what you are thinking. The "Divine Feminine" sounds a bit grand doesn't it? Perhaps a little too mystical for you to get your head around at first, second or third glance? It's not really describing anything concrete to you, other than illustrating that yet again your wife is spouting off spiritual terms which in real life have very little basis in your everyday reality. I can see that.

So let's break this thing down. Who or what is the Divine Feminine Goddess, and what on her green Earth has it got to do with you and me? Do I really believe that there is a Goddess sitting somewhere on a cloud and imbuing all females with some magical, mysterious Divine Femininity? No. I believe that like I believe in a God sitting up there with her. I believe it like I believe in Santa Claus or the tooth fairy. What I do believe in is a spirit, an energy; something that no human can properly contemplate or write about, describe or sum up in even a thousand books. I believe that this energy, this essence is multi-faceted, and that two facets of it are what we know of as male and female.

This is where it can get confusing. This is where you assume that you have God energy, and I have Goddess energy, and that's all there is to it. But that is not how I see it. What I believe is that we both have God and Goddess energy in equal measures. God essence is of course made up of more traditionally masculine traits, and the Goddess essence is more feminine. So as humans we naturally identify ourselves with one or the other. But the truth is that we all have both elements churning around in our souls. You have a whole lotta Goddess in you, Mister, and I've got a dose of God too.

This is probably news to you. It's easy to look at the female form and think, wow, Angelina Jolie is a Goddess. Marilyn Monroe was a Goddess. Naomi Campbell is a Goddess. It's not so easy to realize that the very same Goddess that resides in those iconic females is the same Goddess that sits right smack bang in the middle of your essence also. But she does.

That is what I want you to try to wrap your head around. Because you won't ever understand the Goddess in me until you begin to understand that same energy within you. I believe that as humans this is where we have gone so badly wrong. We have split, divided and, until recently, the males have conquered. Perhaps you fellas are starting to understand or listen to a smidgen of your Goddess side, as in recent times the boundaries haven't been quite so clear.

So how do you embrace your Goddess energy without compromising your masculinity? Well, embracing your Goddess bits won't compromise the bloke in you, I assure you of that. That is a human myth concocted to ensure the continuation of black and white gender roles. This energy is not about stereotypes, it's not about gender, it's not about girls and boys. Rather, it is about the essence of humanity.

Goddess energy, Divine Feminine energy is what is missing from our very God-focused existence. We are all so consumed with creating and materializing things that we have forgotten to nurture what we already have. We have forgotten how to make the most of who we already are. I am not criticizing God energy. It has brought us great things, such as this computer that I write upon, the light shining above my head, jet airplanes and high-heeled shoes. But I fear that the world has become too skewed toward that form of material creativity, and the true inner self of the human race has gone neglected as we strive for something "other", something "man-made", the next fancy gadget or the next year's styles. I want us all to turn our attention to the love of a good woman, to the ability to sit with what we already have and enjoy it without wanting more, spark off it, create from it, internalize it and remember that it is from within that happiness comes, not from without.

The Goddess's divine essence is not about curling your hair and donning lipstick. It's about nurturing, love, caring, compassion and all the traits we wish we had in a mother; just as a divine God energy would be all the traits we would want to have in a perfect father. If we combine the two, then we have a perfect, loving, balanced essence to access both within and without. And in doing so we will strike a better balance, one that comes from an amalgamation of our thoughts, perspective and our feelings. The Goddess will tame the God, just as the God will embolden the Goddess. And in this loving circle we will find each other and ourselves to be complete.

So, husband, where do you go with this fabulous new information? I'm not sure really. It's up to you to consider it and give it the meaning that you feel it deserves. All I would ask is that when worshipping my own Goddess attributes, you turn an inward eye onto your own. Not being a man myself, I cannot tell you what affect this might have on you. But I do believe that you will be helping to make yourself whole.

I am not your other half. The Goddess is. Open yourself up, take a look deep inside, and say hello, inner sister!

Your loving wife.

Alice Grist is author of *The High Heeled Guide to Enlightenment*, the book that charts Alice's journey from party girl to sassy spiritual woman. Alice is also the author of the forthcoming *The High Heeled Guide to Spiritual Living* (2011). Both books are published by O-Books. Alice is the founder and managing editor of Soul-Café (Soul-Café.net), an online network dedicated to "women who know there is more to life than lipstick". On Soul-Cafe Alice regularly interviews and features the spiritual advice and writings of experts and authors. Soul-Cafe provides a safe, happy space for all spiritual seekers. Alice is also a frequent contributor to many magazines and online lifestyle sites, often writing about spirituality in her own quirky, accessible and fierce style. She is a frequent guest on many TV and radio shows. You can also find her on her main website at: web.mac.com/alice-grist/Alice_Grist/Welcome.html

Co-Map Yoni, Heal Hurt, Unleash Pleasure

by Janet Lessin

Little did I know the story that would unravel from my being when I embarked upon my tantric path. I had become "short" with my live-in, snapped at every little thing, then became remorseful and apologetic that I was so ill-behaved. With both my parents precariously at death's door, I knew I was stressed. My sister called and it looked as though Mom would be the first to go. "Get home quick," she said with panicked urgency in her voice.

My partner was an alcoholic with abusive episodes increasing in frequency. I loved him; yet I realized I was enabling him, and I was afraid we would end up some kind of statistic on the front page of the newspaper. I took a boyfriend as refuge, partly from my own personal need and partly from pity. He was "impotent" from being dumped by his girlfriend, my best friend, Jane. She'd made her grand escape from our Hawaiian paradise to Alaska. "Alaska?" I guess it made sense to her.

Tantra had been a "buzz" word repeated to me by many for a number of years. Even boyfriend number two suggested we go to a tantra workshop. He found one and set his sights on the tantra segment of the Loving More (polyamory) Conference in California. I pooh-poohed it. "I don't have the money," I declared.

Fate had another plan. July came, the money "materialized" magically out of thin air; and soon I found myself on the way to meet my destiny. "The Gods must be crazy," I thought; but who was I to question them?

To make a long story short, I found myself sitting across from the tantra teacher. Through another series of unlikely events which fell into place with divine precision, we fell in love, we made love, we cohabited, we married—all by the first week of October.

Still Mother hovered near death; and I fought hard to repress an increasingly nagging, subconscious irritation. "What is repressed soon becomes demonic," the saying goes. I was about to discover how true it was.

I remember how I cried when I was first asked permission to be touched. I recall being totally confused when a tantric lover paused from honoring me (the tantric word for licking the vagina and clitoris) and asked me if he could put on a condom and enter me. I said, "Yes, no, yes, no," and finally a very firm "NO" after a momentary pause to think about what I really wanted. I felt so honored and respected. Until then, I had only been "seduced," and it was assumed that I approved or was ready for touching.

One of my early sacred spot sessions with Sasha touched upon an initial issue. During his honoring of me, he encountered a spot about 6 o'clock inside my vagina which was an "owee." What associations do you have with that pain?" he asked.

I closed my eyes, searching deep within myself. I dismissed the first answer that came to my mind. "Oh, this is too silly, it can't be," I said. My inner Judge had come forth. My Inner Critic was about to censor my words. "Just tell me; it's not silly," Sasha encouraged me.

"When I was small, we used to come home for lunch from school. We didn't have a lot of time to travel, eat, then get back up the hill to school. I would always have to poop and my diet was so poor that I was frequently constipated. My mother would yell outside the bathroom door, "Hurry up! You're going to be late for school!" I would painfully force myself to go, if I could.

Sometimes I would just cry; I couldn't make myself go. My mother would let me stay home and say I was "ill" with an absentee excuse the next day. It was so embarrassing. I had forgotten about all that until now."

Sasha listened and did not make fun of me. "Interesting," he replied. I was no longer tense. My body relaxed and released an ancient pain, an old shame. Sasha moved his hand inside my yoni (vagina). "There. Now how does that feel? Is it still painful in that spot? How about here? No? Now how does it feel here?"

Amazingly, the pain was gone! And I felt free, light! "No," I realized, "there is more." I felt lighter, but not totally light.

Right before Christmas I received the call. "Mom died today. She's gone," my sister reported. It was over. I couldn't afford to go home to Pennsylvania for the funeral. On top of that, I had company coming from the mainland. We live in Maui and when the cold weather comes into "the States" many people like to escape to paradise. My partner Sasha had just spent a year on the road, in exile during a bitter divorce settlement, and had accumulated many "lodging debts" that now demanded reciprocity.

I was newly married, living in a new home on a new island. On top of it all, we defined ourselves as "polyamorists" as well. I had never been actively poly, but had only toyed with the philosophy and had affairs and cheated. But I adjusted.

Sasha and I had a "date" with Sasha's long time lovers, Dan and Jill, two days later. "Should we cancel?" we pondered due to my being in mourning.

"No, I'll be okay," I decided.

The "catalyst" for what was to happen next arrived. I liked Jill immediately. I felt such warmth and love radiating from this delicious being. What a Goddess!

But there was something about Dan I just couldn't put a finger on. I wasn't just not interested and not attracted; I was downright repulsed. Poor Dan. He had done nothing to me; he was quite sweet, with gentle energy and kind eyes.

Later, on our own, Sasha was honoring my yoni. I was going very deep into the sensations. He focused on me for what seemed like hours. I became one with my body after so many years of feeling barely there. I felt all the levels, subtleties and intensities of the different types of orgasms. My mind raced with stories as I sank deeper and deeper into altered states of consciousness, carried there by my beloved devotee who worshiped at my shrine.

All of a sudden, I felt violently ill. I raced to the toilet to vomit. I expelled the "poison." Sasha came into the bathroom and supported me. It all came back to me as my body convulsed and I wretched to free "it" from my throat.

"Oh my God! Tom! Oh my God, he's raping me. He's choking me with his lingam (penis). I can't breathe. I can't breathe. Help! Someone help! He's killing me! Oh my God, someone please stop him, he's killing me!"

The memory of the rape of myself as a 4-year old came forth from the deep recesses of my subconscious mind. My mother had a boyfriend while my father was at work. We would all sit around naked after their lovemaking and laugh. I was a precocious toddler who ran between them. I slipped and fell into Tom's lap, my young lips brushing past his lingam.

I became embarrassed for some unknown reason and ran to my mother. She laughed and held me, reassured me all was fine. I ran back to Tom; he reached for me. I laughed and jumped lovingly into his arms only to be betrayed.

He shoved his huge, erect lingam into my tiny, little-girl mouth. He thrust mercilessly. I had polyps in my nose from allergies, and I had trouble breathing anyway. Now I wasn't getting enough air! I was choking! He was tearing my mouth with the force! He ejaculated. I couldn't breathe! HELP! I was drowning. HELP! I was passing out. No, I was out of my body. I was dead.

I hovered and watched the scene from the ceiling of the room. My mother had been beating on Tom, and he simply ignored her in his lust. I collapsed and hung like a limp doll as he smiled and went "hmmmmm" with blissful delight.

Their focus finally shifted to me. Tom became aware; he

began to respond to my Mom's pounding and screams; but it was too late. They both worked feverishly to revive me, but neither of them had the slightest knowledge of CPR. My mother screamed hysterically, "You've killed my baby! You've killed my baby girl!" Tom smacked her and somehow calmed her, at least for that moment.

"Let's call Marty; I can hear him next door working in the yard." The neighbor was called and seemed to know better what to do. At least he wasn't as distraught as the two of us.

He struggled with my body for a while, but his efforts were fruitless. I looked in amazement at all the fuss below. As they talked, I "noticed" my body and zoomed over to it in my etheric body. I'll never forget how I looked as I gazed down at the form that was myself. It was as if I was a rag doll and was deposited on the floor as such. My left arm was cocked over my head in a 90 degree angle. My right arm was twisted behind my back. I lay face down with my shoulder-length mousy hair all matted up. I was curious, but I don't recall any other emotions that I felt.

"You two have to turn yourselves into the police," Marty whispered softly. "She's gone, June. Face it, she's dead."

My mother let out a piercing wail. She screamed, "No, no, no, no, no!"

The two men calmed her the best they could. After a long discussion, they made the decision to call the police. They turned to leave the room.

Time stood still at that moment. From behind my right shoulder, my "guides" came to take me. They spoke to me in symbols and words not translatable into human language. They showed me the alternative future histories of what was to come if I decided to stay with them. The love I felt was a hundred times any love that humans are capable of feeling here on this plane. It was truly bliss, truly heaven.

They showed me how my mother would be in jail; how she would finally end up in a mental institution. They showed me how my family would suffer; how my father, brother and sister would react, feel ashamed and never quite recover from losing me.

Despite the peace and beauty of all that was offered to me, I didn't give a second thought when I saw what would happen. I no sooner could think, "No thank you; I'm staying" when I found myself rushed back into my body.

I was fully charged with the love of the divine light. Energetically I was still in that next dimension. As I snapped back into place, the force of it bolted my body upright into a standing position. My chakras glowed; my aura intensified with a bright Christ-like light.

"Hello!" I declared with a big grin on my face. Having just touched the face of God himself, I was alive, happy and joyous!

Tom, June and Marty all turned in their tracks at the doorway. They turned and saw me alive after nearly forty-five minutes of being dead. All three screamed and bolted from the room like they had just seen a ghost! They had; and it was me.

I said to myself, "Wow, look what I did to the adults," and giggled. Suddenly, I felt exhausted. I had been vibrating at an intensive level; and just as quickly I settled back into my body and the rhythm of this third-dimensional plane. I found my way to my bed. I fell into a deep slumber. Hours later, my mother cautiously crept back into my room and saw my sleeping form.

I had forgotten what happened for almost forty years. Sasha stayed with me and continued to process until the wee hours of the morning. I was completely destabilized. What I had thought was my life, my childhood, had all been rewritten and had taken on a new meaning. With my mother's death, my psyche had felt "safe" to reveal what lay within.

Poor Dan, he didn't know why I reacted to him so negatively. Here, with a bald head and large ears, he had resembled my perpetrator! My logical mind knew this was a nice person. But my inner child was in panic. "Run away, run away fast," she screamed to me.

Like the layers of an onion, with many layers to go, my healing process had just begun. Even with this memory released, catharsis was only the first step. A few weeks later we "rewired" my primal brain with an alternative program during a Holotropic Breathwork session. That story is for another time.

I never did quite resolve things 100% with Dan. We did manage to go another layer deeper, to connect and even to make love—if only for a brief time. He and Jill are gone now from our lives, perhaps forever. They did not like "processing." Alas, my processing had only just begun.

Sasha and I continue on our journey. I am grateful for his love, devotion and support. I am hopeful that I can now live a full life, free of the internal tortures which affected my health, my life expectancy and my happiness.

I hope in the telling of this intensely personal story that others may see the possibilities for their personal healing. Tantra is a valuable tool of love for the healing of others, for greater depth and intimacy and for sustaining pleasurable sexual connections throughout the duration of any relationship—not just in the early years of sexual discovery, but until death do us part.

Janet Lessin, Professor of Tantric Studies at the School of Tantra, is Center Holder for the Temple of Tantra, a federally-recognized spiritual institution on Maui, Hawaii. She also heads the World Polyamory Association, which hosts the annual Harbin Hot Springs California Tantra and Polyamory conference (www.schooloftantra.net/worldpolyamoryassociation/conferences/HarbinHotSprings2011/HarbinHotSprings2011.html). Janet has written Polyamory: The Poly-Tantra Lovestyle (http://www.schooloftantra.net/Store/Books/PolyamoryManyLoves.htm)

A Journey of Love and Learning

By Nancy Battye

At this time I'm probably at the most evolved point of my own life to date. I've been married twice, the first time at age twenty-three, after dating my former husband for an entire ten days before getting engaged and then married six months later. The marriage in total lasted nine years; although after the first two we were completely miserable with one another. My second marriage lasted five years, and our relationship in total was once again nine years.

The greatest lesson I've learned over the years, with a large amount of past reflection and insight, is that I didn't know myself and was certainly in no position to know or even begin to truly love another person in an intimate way. And in getting to know myself I've come to understand at an even deeper level that what's far more important is the ability to actually love oneself; to have a great level of self-confidence and self-love, and recognize the individual value that we bring to this world.

Sex is sex whether it be good, bad, indifferent, wild sex or great sex. Sex, as I've come to learn firsthand over many years and a wide variety of experiences, is not about making love, until you are indeed connected to who you are in terms of purpose and appreciation for your own higher level of consciousness.

I've lived most of my life not approving of myself and not even aware that I really didn't love myself. I've lived with a number of limiting beliefs by which all I could see at an unconscious level was what my ego mandated me to see: my flaws, my inabilities, my insecurities and my fears. All of those fears and limiting beliefs manifested themselves into the unhealthy relationships I would attract to myself, believing somehow that I deserved to be treated badly. And badly I was treated.

In essence, really, it wasn't the fault of the perpetrators, the men that I was dating or married to. They were simply the vehicles, through their own levels of low self-esteem and insecurities, which I attracted into my life to teach me the lessons that I needed to learn.

After much abuse, disrespect and conflict I eventually began to search deeper into the meaning of what I was experiencing repeatedly in my life. After a lot of focused, intentional and hard work through being committed to the healing process, I have come full circle and begun to live a life where I truly see and recognize my own inherent greatness by virtue of being born a Divine Child of God/Spirit/Universe.

Within that understanding, as I've learned and become accustomed to loving myself, I've attracted into my life a much higher level of kindness, respect and loving interaction from the man who I'm currently with. From this experience I've come to understand and appreciate that truly being loved, making love and being in love with a person who deserves my time and attention is at its core a fundamental aspect of connection and communication through Spirit/Universe/God.

The initial part of the relationship has transformed itself from physical chemistry—which equated to sex for the purposes of a limited physical connection and a way to relieve stress, or at least a minimal way to feel connected to someone—to a place of indescribable Oneness in what is a truly loving act. Our physical union has now given definition to the words "making love", which always seemed to me such an artificial way of making the words "having sex" sound less impersonal. Making love, I now understand, is really about a higher level of communication and connectedness with a soul and spirit who is connected to my own in ways that I can't even begin to express completely.

In order for both men and women to get to a deeply intimate place in which to connect with one another for the purposes of finding deep fulfillment, their level of personal understanding and appreciation of who they themselves are in the puzzle of life has to be ascertained to begin with.

Women and men are both searching for something. More often than not they are probably not completely aware of what that search is for. Perhaps, on some level, they just want to avoid being alone; to feel protected, less lost, to distance the pain of their life experience without really understanding where that pain is coming from.

Women being submissive to the power of men whether in the bedroom or outside of the bedroom is a constant theme, I'm sure, for many women, and for many reasons; even when we think that as women we're strong, independent, resourceful. Oftentimes we really are so weak in so many ways. And it's not that a man needs to fill and define who we are, because we can only do that for ourselves. Until we figure out that that's the core issue in our life, no one else can fix it for us.

Getting in touch with ourselves at the deepest level, in terms of truly accepting, appreciating and loving who we are is one of the fundamental ingredients in entering into and defining a loving relationship with the man of our dreams. Having the security within ourselves will allow us to attract a man who is on the same playing field in terms of their own security and confidence in who they are, and the gifts that they have to offer the world: a true man, a real man, a man who is in touch with his aspirations and contributions to the world, once he's gone through all the various challenges that each decade of life brings to him.

When a man's needs are met and their focus in relationship is to give of themselves fully so that they may be loved and cared for by a woman whose main interest is their genuine happiness, a man will show his true loving nature and character in the manner in which he not only makes love with his woman, but also in the way in which he shows her off to the world, proclaiming his pride in her being at his side.

When a woman knows she can completely trust a man inside and out to care for her, protect her, love her, understand her, respect her and proclaim his unconditional love for her, a woman will then wholeheartedly open up all of who she is to that man in ways that will astound him. Passion will run through every act that she commits for him, as she'll want to be completely available to serve him in loving ways; although ones that still allow her to keep and maintain her independence and her own personal strength in how she interacts with the world.

Once a woman knows that she's truly loved and cared for by a man, who will continually be committed and loyal to her, the depth of love that she will share with that man both in the bedroom and outside of the bedroom will leave him speechless and breathless at the very thought of realizing that there is no greater love than that of a woman.

Trusting in one another, knowing that the other person is always there, unconditionally, to have that person's back protected will allow a depth of sharing, communication and experience in life in which the man will become much more connected with his own feminine side, and correspondingly a woman will be more secure in exploring her more masculine side.

It takes the right relationship to connect with the balance and flow of the feminine and masculine energies. They start off defending their own boundaries, and over time, begin to intermix so easily that it softens and yet at the same time strengthens the bonds between a man and a woman. Once inside of that flow of unconditional love and commitment, each person in the relationship is able to offer more of themselves to each other, and also to the world, knowing that they always have a safe haven in which to be loved, approved of and recognized for their own glorious talents and gifts.

Nancy Battye's mission is to expand the awareness of how having compassion for ourselves and having compassion for others will not only make our lives happier and more joyful, but it will expand the world to a much higher level of joy. She is a spiritual person who is excited about life, ecstatic about the privilege of being a mother to her incredible children and excited to help others recognize the beauty of who they are and their purpose in life. She's a certified diver, an industrious businesswoman, a pet lover, amateur photographer, athletically inclined and a student of success principles. She lives in British Columbia. You can find out more about her at: www.NancyBattye.com

A Woman's Voice

By Andrea O'Loughlin

Quite simply, recognizing my Feminine Divine means to make me visible again—both to myself and to my partner. Many women become invisible over time, losing themselves as they fulfill their roles as wives and mothers. For some, only a life-changing event (in my case, a life-threatening illness now in remission) rips away the façade that all is well and forces us to confront at a very deep level what is truly important in life. At this point, if we are lucky, we rediscover ourselves, our worth, our beauty, our energy—and in that long overdue self-renewal, we seek partners who validate and mirror us in similar ways: intellectually, spiritually and sexually. Men need to see women—really see them—and acknowledge their incredible importance.

As Goddess, I embrace all the passion, wisdom and self-awareness that is the Feminine Divine. Colors are more vibrant, music more intense. All senses are sharpened: touch is subtly nuanced, taste has scent and scent has taste. My heightened awareness burns at an intensity which surprises me. Palpable energy emanates from me and seeks a complementary force. Call it tantra or kundalini energy or universal merging; it is recognizing not just the divine within me, but also the divine within my partner—and together seeking the Divine. Mind you, I'm new to all of this. I am still learning and seeking. While that makes me a novice, it also engenders wonder and enthusiasm, exploring possibilities, seeking someone just as intense, just as willing to connect soul to soul.

I don't presume to speak for all women. But this is what I seek...

First and foremost, I desire equality. No more shushing or

silencing as past partners have done; such things kill the spirit. No topic is taboo as we bare our souls, each to the other. Let's talk about everything: film, books, sexuality, world hunger, positive change. Admittedly, this is an exquisite risk, but ultimately so rewarding as we drop traditional male/female roles of dominance/submissive and embrace equity. My male partner mirrors some of my feminine qualities such as gentleness. But he also exudes strong male energy that draws me like a magnet. Again, it is complementary energy that merges and multiplies when we meet. Because he listens to me and values me as an equal, I am open to him.

Second, understand that sexuality depends upon intellect and spirituality. If we cannot connect on those levels, sex is merely a cheap diversion. To enter me physically is to enter my mind and soul. At its best, making love sends energy through fingertips and spines, recognizes the divine in one another, and connects to the Divine Source. Not every meeting results in fireworks. But every meeting is being present in the moment, understanding the depth and the extraordinary gift we've been given—to know one another at such an intimate level that we can make love with our eyes and our hearts open. We appreciate the "extraordinary ordinary." It is nothing short of total mind-body-spirit connection.

Finally, we have fun and enjoy life. We laugh, dance and play. We are friends as well as lovers. We maintain our own voices even as we share moments of absolute and profound unity, and the Universe smiles at our Divine Balance. I have waited a lifetime for this relationship. My promise is this:

Give me my voice, and I'll give you my heart.

Andrea Kay O'Loughlin lives in the Midwest of the United States and shares her passion for literature—especially poetry—with her students. Confronted with a life-threatening illness (sarcoidosis), she turned away instinctively from Western medicine, pursuing instead Eastern alternative therapies such as yoga, meditation and massage. Now in remission, she has rediscovered herself, embraced wholeness, seeks mind-body-spirit balance, and only recently has discovered tantric/kundalini energy. She is passionate about life and embraces "extraordinary ordinary" moments. Andrea welcomes questions and dialogue at: akolough@earthlink.net

How to Love a 21st Century Goddess

By Dashama Konah

I imagine it was much simpler in the old days, when a woman had a defined role in society, primarily to make babies and cook meals for her family. Those were the patriarchal times that women eventually grew tired of and rebelled against, fighting for the right to vote and have jobs, of all things. As society shifted, through great struggles and adversity, women have evolved to a level of "equality" within our western societies that is celebrated by women and tolerated by men.

What has this done for the dating scene and relationships? This is of the biggest concern to me. I have witnessed in my own life a fervent independence and desire to be self sufficient, perhaps to my own detriment, at times. I have seen this same strength shine radiantly from many modern Goddesses whom I know and am proud to call my friends.

The common Goddess conversation typically revolves around the lack of available and worthy men. I hate to admit it, but it is the most prevalent topic amongst single Goddesses that I know.

Perhaps the reason these Goddesses are single is they find no man worthy of their time and love? Or conversely, perhaps there is some legitimacy to this observation that has a deeper root? This leads to the question: what makes a man worthy of a Goddess, which can be conveyed to him so that he might be able to step into the role of the King that we seek?

Well, first of all, yes, I imagine men can be taught how to embody their divinity and step up as the masterful beloved and King of our hearts, if he's willing. So how to court a modern day Goddess?

This is a point of debate for many women. Depending upon

one's interests and upbringing, the answer can vary greatly. For some, exotic adventures of travel and play make the most memorable first dates. For others, fabulous live music and dancing all night create the ambiance necessary to get to know a potential suitor.

Dinner and a movie is almost certainly a no-no, by all stretches of the imagination. This is the most uncreative date and should be avoided at all costs. Be creative! At least a picnic on the beach with some champagne and raw chocolate allows for intimacy, creativity and sensational pleasure to abound, encouraging a deeper understanding of the Goddess of your desire.

Whatever you choose to do for this special first encounter, be certain it is not left to her to decide. Goddesses love Kings who are decisive, confident and know what they want! Be forward, speak from your heart and express your heart's desire. At the same time, don't be pushy, assertive or needy; these will turn her away quickly.

She loves some mystery. A little challenge is a good thing. And most importantly, call her directly! Text messages say: "I don't really care about you enough to call" or else "I'm afraid of rejection, so a text feels safer". These are signs of a coward and will certainly indicate certain aspects of your confidence level, so be bold, and pick up the phone. When her sweet voice picks up and speaks with the honey dripping from her lips, you will be so glad you took the leap.

Ask her what she likes. What makes her happy? Get to know who she truly is; not just what she does, where she's been…but who she is on the inside. And when communicating, express back to her what you understand to be true about what you feel she is expressing. This will help her to know you are listening! *There is no greater flattery than to let a Goddess know you have been listening to her when she is speaking*!

To truly listen is an art form that seems to have been lost long ago. When you demonstrate the ability to listen, you let someone know you care. And that is a deep and beautiful gift you can give for free and with great ease. Give this gift often and generously, even if the topic is of little interest to you! You will soon find that it is not the topic that you are listening to, but the vibration of her heart's desires, her dreams and challenges being expressed. Be compassionate and love her despite her shortcomings. Forgive her for her faults, and she will do the same for you. Be kind and compassionate to her family and friends, for they mean the world to her, regardless of what she may say!

A few key elements to a worthy mate, for most Goddesses I know, include: Knowing how to worship the Goddess both in and out of bed… How to care for her in times of need, while allowing for her independence simultaneously… He must be a provider, despite what the feminists suggest, since a Goddess should not have to slave away to put food on the table and pay rent… A worthy King is fun, creative, imaginative and enjoys dancing… Laughter is a requirement in the home and life of the Goddesses, so her King must be able to crack a joke or two at least! Throw off the heavy burden of life as they cross the threshold of the home and enter into the magical world she has created for them to enjoy… A King enjoys travel and adventure, as much as cuddling on the couch to a great romantic comedy… He should be active physically, a leader and an inspiration that encourages daytrips to the mountains or walks along the beach… A man who decisively knows what he wants, and moves confidently and boldly in the direction of his dreams… A King who enjoys the support and conversation of his Goddess and is free and open with sharing his emotions.

In the bedroom, he should be gentle, playful and inventive, and open to suggestions and excited about trying new things: for example, breath-centered present-moment awareness in tantric love sessions set to exotic music in candle-lit rooms. Hot massage oil, fragrance and rose petals, raw chocolate, champagne and strawberries contribute to a delicious love session fit for a

Goddess adorned in silk robes and gemstones. Peel the layers away, and she offers herself completely with no hesitation, as they bow to each other in humble devotion and adoration.

The feeling of adoration should be mutual and exclusive, not shared with others in daytime affairs. Her mind must rest at ease knowing he will be true to her heart. This trust is the lifeblood of their union, without which all else crumbles like dry stones on a hot fire pit, turning to ash and dissolving into nothingness.

How do you keep a Goddess, once you have courted her and won her heart?

This is simple: don't change what you were doing in the beginning to win her heart! All too often I hear the same sob story about Goddesses who are courted by snakes disguised as Kings. They fake who they are to win her heart; and then when they know they have her tied down, whether through marriage, children or long term commitment, they reveal their true colors. These true colors are oftentimes completely opposite from the colors they were parading around with during the courtship phase. This is totally unacceptable and should be completely banned forever. Why would a man want to trap a Goddess into thinking he is one way, when he is really something the exact opposite? It sounds quite absurd, but it actually happens all the time.

A friend of mind told me she was married twenty years before she discovered the man she had wed. She was so busy all those years raising their children, she had not quite realized who he was. It wasn't until after the children had left the house to attend college, that she found herself living with what appeared to be a complete stranger! He didn't enjoy long walks on the beach, as he had pretended to enjoy during their three year courtship. He preferred golf on TV to spending time outside. She loathed the TV and never would have turned it on if it wasn't for his insistence. The list of fraudulent actions was long, and unfortunately this happens all too often.

He must be who he truly is and love her for who she really is. There's nothing worse than two people both trying to change each other into someone else who would be much better suited for them. Best to just let it go from the beginning, and leave the door open for someone else who will be the perfect fit.

Be authentic. Be who you are. Don't hold anything back or pretend to be someone in hopes to win someone's heart. In the end, the hearts will be broken and the time wasted. Although there is always opportunity to grow and learn from these relationship dramas, its best for all involved if we enter into union authentically and with no false fronts or pretenses.

When you have won the heart of a Goddess, it is because there is true love, admiration, adoration, mutual respect and a shared vision for the present and for the future together. That combination is a rare occurrence and is well worth the waiting and sifting through potential partners, until the glass slipper is presented in just such divine timing that it is unmistakable and ready to be explored deeper.

It must be noted that fairy tales should not be expected, as the reality of life is far too precious to live in the illusion of perfection. From time to time, there may be disagreements, and seeing eye-to-eye may be a challenge at times. This is to be expected and embraced. Know that the challenges are growth opportunities and can lead to a deeper understanding of one another. Cherish these opportunities and love better, deeper and more fully as a result.

Above all, approach each moment, in the present moment, with no expectations, attachments or judgment and you will always live in a field of pure potentiality, infinite possibility and expanded awareness. In this field of pure being, deep, resonant frequencies of love and joy, bliss and divine sensual sacred union abound. Dive into that ocean and swim in the warm currents of Ma Shakti, and be forever transformed by her wisdom, grace and all-embracing love. Honor the Supreme Goddess and she will, in turn, honor the Divine One within you as well.

Dashama Konah Gordon, based in both Los Angeles and Miami, is an internationally known teacher, author and lifestyle coach, founder of the Global 30 Day Yoga Challenge, Perfect 10 Lifestyle online community, Yoga for Foster Children, and Pranashama Yoga Institute. Her powerful message has reached millions of people around the world through video, online and print media. Dashama is a teacher of teachers and travels the world offering yoga certification trainings courses and retreats. You can find out more about her on her websites: www.dashama.com, 30dayyo gachallenge.com/ and perfect10lifestyle.com/.

Merger

By Amanda Lyons

So, you desire to know a Goddess? To delve into all her spaces and allow her to awaken every cell in your body? Really and truly? With the depth of pure sincerity?... Or with the shallowness of a passing phase? Do you have the time to give to her while she moves through her layers of protection, passing through vulnerability and entering the depths of Goddess sensuality?

You see, to really know a woman, you have to give her your time, to be patient as she senses into you and decides... is this for real? You have to give her your attention, be present to the point that she feels your presence as clearly as she would feel your body pressing against hers. You have to stand centered in your power, so that she can feel your support and sense the safety of your enveloping energy. She knows when your mind has switched focus; she knows when you are there with her physically but thinking of someone else, or of work, football, what your mates are doing right then...and in that moment, you have lost her. She may allow you to go ahead with the motion, each of you enjoying a few moments of physical release, just for the sake of the orgasm. But you will have missed the chance of *knowing* her.

The Essence of Merger

At one time I believed that a female's natural energy and emanation was of passive calmness, the quiet, kind nurturer, essentially at peace and still. And that the energy of a man was aggressive, outward, noisy and chaotic, with the competitive drive of masculinity creating havoc in order to leave its mark like a scorch in the earth. In the realms of ego and personality, this could be a true representation of what women and men are—if, that is, we allow ourselves to sweep the paint brush of generalization over the picture and don't mind the subsequent blurring.

Following several years of working with healing and yoga, and tuning into the essences of male and female, I now feel very differently. Instead, I see it that the masculine essence (whether in a male or female body) is stillness itself, a calm awareness of its own existence, of its own power and perceptive abilities. It is supremely serene in the space of "I Am I Am I Am". It exudes confidence without the need or desire to prove itself and without any staining of competitive arrogance. It feels like a warm and silent, safe haven.

The female essence on the other hand is in fact *chaos* itself! It moves and changes and destroys and gives birth. It creates with the sole purpose of destroying in order to refresh, recreate, rebirth something new into existence for just a little while. It is a flowing and pouring of love and sensuality, a reaching out and grasping, a setting free and running free, dancing free to the rhythm of nature and the beat of life… and death. It is the understanding and accepting of cycles, the expression of desire. It can be agonizingly beautiful or vengefully vile, depending on what is needed to keep the natural flow and order alive.

Regardless of whether we are male or female, we all have a blend of these essences flowing through us. It is rare for us to have exactly half and half measures of male/female essence, and it is our individual blend of these that contributes to creating our uniqueness. The contorting nature of essence means that either one can bubble to the surface to allow us to deal with many varied life situations. For example, it is common for a mother to draw more on her masculine essence of stability and authority in order to guide or discipline her child, even if at most other times she is the embodiment of the feminine. In fact, it is easy to fall out of touch with our core essence when life throws challenges our way that demand an outward expression of our naturally less dominant state of being.

True Gifting

One of the greatest gifts we can give each other through sexual union is the opportunity for us to reconnect with our core. As a woman who has to draw on her masculinity in many areas of life, my deepest desires and my need to reconnect with my femininity is best met by a partner who, during our intimate moments, is strong in his masculine essence. Of course, there are also many women who need to reconnect with their masculine core, and men who long to allow their feminine being free expression. Partners who are complimentary opposites within their energetic selves have an amazing potential for fulfilling, devotional gifting—for enabling the soul of each to surface in sweet ecstasy… *if* they allow one another to move beyond the empty-grunting-humping-over-in-a-flash sex, and into a deeper experience of physical union. If they delve within so that they can know themselves fully, know their essence, then they can resurface more whole, and allow the merger of Goddess and God.

Sex is great. It's sweaty and noisy and fun for the most part, and a fantastic way to burn a few calories. It's a wonderful way to spend time with someone while enjoying the physicality of each other's bodies, allowing fantasies to run free in the mind and in the bedroom and to get in touch with our animal instinct and raw heated passion, with the added bonus of an orgasm or two.

Love-centered, sacred sexual union, on the other hand, is a different experience. It is to die in passionate beatitude, touch heaven's gateway, hear the angels singing your glory, and to be reborn into the newness of life. Now that really *is* "Good Lovin'"… But it doesn't begin and end with the physical act of sex itself.

Bedrock

In *The Aquarian Teacher* Yogi Bhajan tells us that "sex does not just happen in bed" (or in the kitchen, on the sofa, back of the car, you name it). "It starts in day-to-day life". Foreplay is not a few short seconds of fumbling fingers and hurried licks. It includes the way in which we greet one another after a day at work; the kindness and generosity we share when we prepare food; the "thank you" and acknowledgement when that kindness has been received; the smiles and cute little kisses we share while washing the pots; and in the attention we show as we listen to one another talk, truly listening, instead of half-listening while continuing to read the paper or feed the cat.

All of this, given freely from the heart, lends itself to forming the perfect foundation on which the woman will lie and open herself to the man's longing. It is the bed of mutual respect and kindness that allows both man and woman to feel connected to, and safe with each other. It is the bedrock that allows the bed to veraciously rock!

Men be warned though, she will know if the gifts you give are delivered purely with the motive of getting your own needs met. If you give falsely, without genuine loving kindness, she will close off to you. And while your piston works up a steam, she will be off in her mind, dreaming a different dream.

Dream a Little Dream

Millions of songs from every conceivable genre are fuelled by it, with lyrics and melodies pulling at heart-strings and fanning the flames of our sexual desire. Poets have dedicated centuries worth of words to it. Pages and pages of wisdom, tradition and philosophy have attempted to teach us, guide us on our journey to and through it. And yet the only way we are ever going to know the power of it is to experience it first hand, our own merger, melt-down and submission in the heat of it… "It" being the blissful Divine union between man and woman, between souls, and between Earth-bound humans and the infinite consciousness.

This is my own dream, manifested into reality…

There is space between us. Unseen stirrings swirl the air in that space as we gaze into the portals of our souls. We consciously link our breath… Inhale… Exhale… Deepening and softening the flow… In... Out... You begin to drink in my body with your eyes, slowly observing the curves of my throat, neck, breasts and hips. I plunge into a mystifying mix of coy vulnerability and heightened desirous passion, as my skin flushes pink… In this moment the choice must be made, how safe is this? Do I trust you? Can I allow myself to open fully, to expose the gateway to my inner sanctuary and allow you to enter? I breathe deeper, soften, center. I sense into your energy…

I perceive the strength of your presence. In you I see stillness, the unerring master of consciousness itself. My soul recognizes this place, remembers it from eons past and finds within the folds of your spirit, her home. Yes. I trust.

Moving towards one another, not quite touching, our lips draw close. I feel your heated breath on my upturned face. I breathe you in… Skin tantalizingly near to touching, within the gap tingles of lust spark like electricity between us. The yearning for contact is pushed beyond our limits of resistance and we fall into each other's fervent embrace. Fingertips stroke with tenderness and slowness along the fullness of each of our bodies. From head to each individual toe we caress, explore, tease and awaken every part, making it known unto itself. I close my eyes and acutely feel my body's reaction to your attention. I surrender into you, knowing the only bruises you will cause are the pleasurable bruises of groins pressing on hips. My heart is safe with yours.

My senses awaken, feeling and being felt, seeing and being seen, inhaling the sweet musky scents, tasting the salty moisture on glistening skin, listening to your softly spoken words, hearing the sighs and groans of delectation and responding with gasps of pure bliss. Every part of you becomes entwined with every part of me… Creating connection. The heat rises as does my pelvis, lifting towards you, begging for your mouth's ministration, longing for your tongue's wet softness. Our hands feverishly grasp, limbs interwoven as our craving to be even closer intensifies. Hearts pound, groins throb, souls cry out for ecstatic merger. Looking up to your face as you bear down on me, arms like towers holding me in place… I see you.

Beyond this physicality, curiously beyond mere physical sensation, a subtle shift occurs…

I see you.

In this space I am humble before you, devoted to you. You are the God to my Goddess, and without the loss of my own regal Self, I relinquish my ego-self to you. Unspoken permission is given: take me now. Take me into your keep, take me out of this world and into another, take me deeply, fully, so I can melt and merge into the Oneness with you.

Animalized raw passion sounding out from our lips and driving you harder, deeper, faster. Yes, yes, **YES!** Our wildest earthiest natures take our pairing deep to the core of humanness... fuck me, FUCK ME… before propelling us like lightning into the realms of the unseen… I forget to breathe. Within the fire of frenzy, as if in slow and rapturous motion, I enter the trance of ecstasy with you, and for fleeting seconds that feel like infinity itself, we are with God. We are the Universe.

We lay together in silent stillness. Only our breath moves whilst our spirits realign with Earth once more. Hot flesh begins to cool as would embers in their hearth; sweated skin touching sweated skin, the echo of passions shared. Sighing softly, I press my face into your chest as your fingers continue to play me, caressing, following the curvature of my spine, sending divine tingles around my already tingling body. Our eyes shine with love refreshed; bodies remain entwined, our bond complete…

Now it is time to sleep.

So, you desire to know a Goddess? To delve into all her spaces and allow her to awaken every cell of your body? Really and truly? Then, please… Re-connect with your true core. And learn to know your own awakened God potential within.

Amanda Lyons is a holistic therapist, facilitator and kundalini yoga teacher with over 20 years of experience in therapy work and a life-long interest in spirituality, particularly in how to use spiritual philosophy as a foundation in all relationships. Amanda offers her services to both men and women with a wide range of needs, yet has found that her work often takes her into the realms of relationships, esteem-building and empowerment. For more information on Amanda and her work please go to: www.angelsandblossom.co.uk

What the Hades is Going On in the Celestial Temple of Love??

A story by Lyvea Rose

It's 2011 and I'm an educated, forty-something woman with yoganini thighs. Hurray for me! I'm living in a funky suburb in a cushy western city. Hurray again! I'm also single. Not so hurray.

Rumor has it that if I want to re-activate my love life, I need to rediscover my sexual essence. The feminine core of me. You see, I'm one of those women who gave up on men, woke up my inner Mars, and marched out to hunt the f*#cking mammoth myself. I figured it was more efficient than the alternative: having to spend all day, every day, being a super-empathic mummy substitute with supernatural cleaning skills, so that some kindly old patriarch would feel inspired to build a roof over my head and provide me with a lifetime supply of gluten-free muffins.

(I wouldn't ever hurt a mammoth, honestly.)

But hang on a minute; what the Hades has happened to my inner Venus? *Hallo-o-o, anyone home?* And come to think of it...what has happened to all the men?

To find out, I lie down, close my eyes, and astral travel out of my apartment and over to the Celestial Temple of Love. Here's what I see...

* * *

Mars: (*Running around in the nude*) Holy ram's horns, where's my suit of armor? I'm sure I left it on the floor here somewhere. (*Calls out*) Venus, honey, have you seen my armor?

Venus: (*Reclining on the bed*) I am the source of love that dissolves your armor, darling.

Mars: But I need it! I can't go out like this!

Venus: You look divine, darling. Who are you fighting, anyway?

Mars: Oh, you know, the usual troublemakers. The people that don't understand me; the people that don't give me what I want; the people who fail to admire me. Same as always.

Venus: How about a nice long walk through the gardens of paradise, instead? How about a whole day of tantric pleasure? How about I sit in your lap and we dissolve together into infinite bliss?

Mars: Sure, honey. Can't wait. But I've just got to go out and prove a few things first.

Venus: (*Stomping off to climb into her sea-shell bathtub…*) If I had known how busy you were going to be fighting all your battles, I never would have run away with you! I'm lonely!

Mars: (*Rushing to her and kissing her*) How can you be lonely? I always come home in the end, don't I? How about you spend the day generating a whole lot of gorgeous, sexy, feminine vibes, and I'll join you at twilight?

Venus: I guess you're right. I'm way too evolved to cry over you. In fact, I'm not even going to miss you. I've got a lot of magnetizing to get on with. I'm going to magnetize myself a magnificent day. A day full of music, dancing and laughter. And I'm going to magnetize a whole bunch of muses to play with. There will be joy and beauty and pleasure and…

Mars: God, that sounds *great!* I wonder...Maybe I'll stay home today and hang out with you and your muses?

Venus: Hmmm... I'm not sure. If you're going to be restless, I don't want you around.

Mars: No, no; I've changed my mind. I want to be here with you. I want to hang out and relax and play. I want to make love to you. (*He gets in the bathtub with her.*) Honey, have I ever told you I'm yours for all eternity?

Venus: Yes, darling, but tell me again.

Mars: Only if you tell me what you've done with my armor...

Venus: Oh...Well...Umm...(*Softly*) I buried it.

Mars: You WHAT?!

Venus: I buried it.

Mars: WHAT THE HADES FOR?!

Venus: You don't need it.

Mars: But there's so much I want to do! How can I go out without my armor?

Venus: How can you make love to me IN your armor?

Mars: I CAN'T BELIEVE YOU BURIED IT!

Mars leaps out of the bath, rushes outside and starts digging up the garden of paradise. He digs and digs and digs.

After a thousand years or so, Venus wanders outside to find him. He's sitting on the ground, staring up at the sky with a look of fierce concentration.

Venus: Found it yet?

Mars: Shhhh! I'm magnetizing.

Venus: Fantastic! So-o-o much nicer than fighting! And what are you magnetizing?

Mars: *(Grumpily)* A new suit of armor.

Venus sighs and starts dancing around him. Mars sulks at first. But after another thousand years or so, he gets to his feet and begins to dance with her. Immediately, the garden is filled with musicians. Friends arrive with gifts; chefs begin to cook up a feast; flowers burst into bloom on the vines.

And at long last, Mars realizes that it's much more fun to hang out with Venus than strut around in his armor making sure that everyone in the village still knows who he is. (The best.)

But then one morning, Venus is woken up by a terrible sound. It's like torture! The bathtub tap is dripping.

Venus: *(Nudging Mars)* Darling, wake up. You gotta fix that tap. It's driving me bonkers.

Mars: Huh?

Venus: DARLING, YOU GOTTA FIX THAT TAP!

Mars: *(Turning over)* Stop bothering me. I'm way too busy surrendering to the Divine Feminine.

While Mars snores and gurgles like a sweet baby cherub, Venus lies awake in bed. And that's when she begins to wonder if Mars still has a purpose in life, besides loving her. She realizes she WANTS him to have a purpose that has NOTHING to do with her—and everything to do with creating maximum freedom in his life...And in his soul.

The next morning, the tap is still dripping.

Mars: (*Waking up suddenly*) F*#CKING TAP!

He hurls himself out of bed and digs his tool box out from under the tantric altar (it's propping up the leg that fell off). With a determined grunt, he fixes the tap in one second flat. Excellent, he thinks to himself. And then he takes a long look around the temple. There's a window latch that's broken, so he fixes that. And there's a globally-friendly business to run. He sits at his desk and starts working.

From the bed, Venus watches. Oh my Goddess, she thinks to herself, a purposeful man with a glint of freedom in his heart is VERY SEXY.

Venus: *(Quietly)* Yum...Come here.

Mars: Hang on a bit, honey. Got some stuff to do, you know.

Venus: *(With a sigh of contentment)* Okay, darling.

Mars: (*Turning to her*) Yeah...? You mean that? IS EVERYTHING FINALLY OKAY?

Venus: Yeah, everything is finally okay. Now come back to bed.

Mars works for quite a while, gets heaps of stuff done, and then throws himself down beside Venus and ravishes her all the way to infinity. And obviously it's the best love-making the galaxy has ever witnessed. Supernovas burst spontaneously with delight, the moon forgets to set, and all the stars within a thousand-light-year radius take a peek.

* * *

I came back to Earth with a thud and landed on my sofa. And it seemed that I'd picked up a passenger from the temple—because Venus lay with me, entangled in my arms. She was naked, and her hair fell across my face. Her limbs were supple, and her pussy was golden. And then slowly, she dissolved. She soaked right into me, and took me over.

Not knowing what to do, I went for a walk. I admired myself in the shop windows, had a coffee, and when I got back home I rang a few friends. "Venus is back", I told them calmly… And then I dropped the phone, because someone behind me was saying, "Look out!" and grinning and wrapping his arms around me, ready or not.

Oh, you know, it wasn't anything too weird: just that man I'd been seeing recently in my dreams.

And I *was* ready... At least I *think* I was.

"And if you aren't, too bad", whispered Venus.

The man agreed with her, I could tell.

Lyvea Rose is an astrologer, counselor, and columnist. She has been published on the web, and in newspapers and magazines. She writes horoscopes for the Psychic Club of Australia, and is now working on her first (funny) book about the stars. You can book an in-depth, personal reading and healing with Lyvea, or subscribe to her newsletter/forecasts, at www.lyvearoseastrology.com

Sacred Communion

By Elaine Caban

Even though the act of sex comes quite naturally to both men and women, we can often become insecure, confused and frustrated with "mastering" this process. And really, the main point of confusion is that sex is not a process at all. We see so many "How To" books, videos, magazine articles, etc., suggesting that they can transform any man or woman into an amazing lover. Mostly out of curiosity, I have read many of these, and inevitably end up shaking my head in sadness and dismay.

Creating an amazing sexual experience for yourself and your lover has very little to do with the latest (or even ancient) techniques, endurance or fancy props. It has EVERYTHING to do with tapping into your Beloved's own sexual "energy" and learning how to work with that "flow" of energy that already exists in both of you. In order to make the experience **mind-blowing**, one must actually leave the mind—and enter into Sacred Communion, where nothing else exists but the two of you, as spiritual beings, transported beyond the mere human realm.

Any couple, despite their level of spiritual knowledge, can experience a true Sacred Communion—one that leaves them detached from their bodies, and instead interconnected with their Beloved. I learned a powerful ritual from my own tantric teacher, Michael Mirdad, and have since added a few modifications based on my personal experiences.

The first step to moving into a Sacred Communion is TRUST. A woman must know, upon entering an act of communion that her needs are going to be met, in every way, BEFORE the man's, rather than the other way around. Why? Because men heat up and climax faster than women. And too often the man simply does his thing, experiences his release, and then the woman is left unsatisfied, having barely been aroused and certainly not satisfied.

By establishing this trust, a woman can then relax and surrender to her Beloved, without having to worry about being left with a quick experience where she neither climaxed nor had a genuinely "intimate" connection. Surrender is crucial to this communion. If either lover isn't willing to fully surrender and be vulnerable, then the process may in the end be pleasurable in a shallow way—but it will never be taken to the heightened level of true INTIMACY. In-to-me-see.

When it comes down to it, more than anything else we all simply desire intimacy. For a man, this should be a relief, because it does not require any fancy tactics or in-depth know-how. And things like your size or stamina play a very minor role. However, true intimacy, which can really only be obtained through being vulnerable, terrifies most people, both men and women—or at the very least baffles them.

So let me suggest that you simply make an effort to SLOW down, tap into your Sensual nature, and let that lead the way. As a couple, you must first begin by setting aside at least one day or night a week to honor one another. Neither of you may deviate from this date or break it, unless an emergency gets in the way. Make it the utmost priority.

In order to make this communion Sacred, you must prepare your Sacred Space. Make sure the area, which will most likely be your bedroom, is clean and clutter free. Light candles or incense, and play soft music in the background. You should also run a warm, candle-lit bath, perhaps with sea salt and rose petals in it.

This ritual begins by ceremoniously removing one another's clothing. It is crucial not to rush this part. Make sure that you are both standing in front of each other, and that you have permission to unveil one another. One at a time, slowly remove each article of one another's clothing. First, the man undresses the woman. Then the woman undresses the man. As each article of clothing is removed, stop and gaze at the newly uncovered body part with adoration. This is your partner's TEMPLE and it should be honored each and every time as though you are seeing it for the first time.

Very Important Note: this is not necessarily a prelude to having SEX. The removal of the clothing is symbolic of removing all security blankets and armor that we have often placed around ourselves in order to keep from becoming vulnerable or exposed. When we are standing before one another naked, we become exposed and fragile. Yet it is ONLY in this state that we are able to TRULY MERGE and become ONE. Also, in our Nudity, we are at our most BEAUTIFUL state of GLORY! The EGO has told us that we should conceal and cover up our Nakedness, especially by reminding us of all our mistakes and failures, or even worse, by reminding us of times in the past when we were exposed and then got hurt. I challenge you to rise above your EGO and choose a new perspective.

Once you have removed each other's clothing, you move into the bathtub. Water has been used in sacred ceremonies for centuries. It is a sign of cleansing, renewing and purifying. By bathing one another, you are preparing your temples to be worshiped. Slowly bathe one another, taking time to wash each other's beautiful bodies and hair. Be very sensual in this act. You can also massage one another in the water with massage oil. Slowly dry one another with a towel, and then move back into the bedroom.

Sit naked on the bed directly across from one another in a meditative pose with legs crossed, on a pillow if needed. Your knees can be touching one another's, or else slightly separated. Gaze softly into each other's eyes. Place both of your hands on your heart and simply repeat "Namaste" out loud to one another. (*Namaste*, a word in Hindi, a language of India, means "hello". But it also means "I bow to the Divine in you".)

Feel Divine Love radiating from within as you say this sacred word. Now, place your RIGHT hand on your Beloved's heart, while maintaining eye contact, and have them do the same. Take a few deep breaths together. Once your breath is synchronized, consciously send each other Divine Love, from one heart chakra to the other. Feel your heart filling up with LOVE. And then visualize the energy as a brilliant PINK LIGHT transferring from your heart to your partner's. Be sure to keep your heart OPEN, so it can both RECEIVE and GIVE LOVE at the same time. Continue sending and receiving Divine Love, while maintaining eye contact for at least a few minutes. This might sound like a simple, subtle, even cheesy exercise, but it can actually be VERY powerful and evoke deep feelings of Love and Oneness.

Now, lower your hands and place them in front of your heart space, as though you are praying. Look into each other's eyes in a soft gaze. Set out the intention to see ONLY the Highest form of this person that sits before you. SEE beyond each other's physical body, what you know of them, their past, your past experiences with them, their failures, successes... look beyond any attachment you have towards them—including romantic attachment. SEE them as nothing but PURE LIGHT. Gaze into each other's eyes and FEEL the presence of the Divine. Ask your partner to do the same for you. It is crucial that you are both intentionally seeing beyond one another's physical form.

Once you have done this, picture your SOULS, which are the only things to focus on at this moment, MERGING. Literally feel your two Spirits becoming ONE. You may want to say something like "We now choose to MERGE into ONE BE-ing" so that you are both in sync with one another and with the merging. Maintain eye contact as you consciously Merge into each other's Soul. Look into each other's eyes DEEPLY—and know that the person you are looking at is your OWN reflection...and even more than that, the reflection of the Divine.

Once this in-depth Spiritual Merging takes place, you can then slowly begin to physically merge your bodies. You may want to embrace each other, and land soft kisses all over each other. You can stroke the face, run your fingers through the hair, flick your tongue on their skin. Make sure to be very conscious of your movements. Move and breathe slowly and rhythmically, never breaking physical contact. Perhaps have some heated massage oil nearby, so that you can exchange slow, sensual massages. Remember, every time you touch each other's bodies, you are worshiping that person's Temple. Do so with great intention and adoration. Do not touch any erogenous zones at this point. This is about experiencing INTIMACY. If you immediately start arousing one another, you won't last very long. You must get in the habit of using physical touch as a means of worshiping, and not just pleasuring.

Remember that the person before you is an image, a manifestation of God/Goddess—and deserves to be treated and worshiped like one. When you touch each other's bodies, do so with the greatest honor and glory. You should both be humbled and honored in the highest form, simply for the opportunity to physically worship one another. Touch each other's body as though they were made of pure gold and gemstones. When you touch your partner's skin, FEEL the pleasure that they themselves are feeling from being worshiped. You have MERGED into ONE Spiritual Being—so what you do to your partner, you also do to yourself, and vice-versa.

As you worship him/her and recognize their Divinity, so too, do you worship yourself. It is imperative to make this connection. By doing so, you will both receive more pleasure and spiritual growth than you could have ever anticipated. You will also begin to treat each other differently all-around. Once you both realize that what you do to ONE, you do to yourself, you will speak differently to each other, and treat each other differently. You will be so attuned with each other's pain and pleasure, that you will be walking around as ONE Spirit.

It is up to both of you to decide whether to continue on and have intercourse. What you have done up until this moment is true lovemaking itself. I encourage you both to do this ritual on occasion, without the intercourse or sexual orgasms, to help break the habitual patterns of meaningless sex that many couples fall into routinely.

Once you do move into actual intercourse, the lovemaking should remain just as sacred. If there is one thing my teacher Michael Mirdad has taught me, the key to maintaining this spiritual connection is to SLOW DOWN... especially when actually penetrating. By slowing down, you will be able to feel more—both of you—and you will also be able to remain more deeply in the present moment.

When a man is penetrating a woman, it is natural to want to "thrust" himself into her, strong, fast and hard. But keep in mind that when doing this, he is quite literally slamming into her, and all of her sexual organs. It is not pleasurable, no matter how much she moans or tells you it is—yes, we have been conditioned to tell white lies in order to please our partners.

Would you kiss her the same way? No (or at least hopefully not). When kissing a woman, a man takes his time and savors it. The human mouth is a very delicate erogenous zone. Men seem to understand this, which is why the kiss is done slowly and sensually. News alert!—women have other erogenous zones, one of which is her other set of lips, and it is just as delicate as the first.

When you pound ferociously into it, she is unable to feel true pleasure and both of you will be unable to keep that rhythmic, attuned soul connection. When I say to slow down, I do not mean just a little. I mean to the point where you are moving just a little bit faster than not moving at all. Be sure that you do not stop, though, and try to keep the motion fluid.

After a few minutes, you will find a mutual rhythm between

your pelvis and hers… and once you do, what happens next can be Magical. It will seem as though you are dancing. You can switch from keeping your body tightly pressed up against hers as you dance, to slowly pulling your head up so that you are staring into one another's eyes as you move. There is no need to stay in one position either, so long as the rhythm remains slow and fluid. You can move her legs around, come from behind or slide her on top of you. These position changes should remain slow and fluid as well, and you should frequently gaze into each other's eyes. Eye gazing can give you a dual pleasure, especially when penetration is occurring, because you can feel both your souls merging at the same time that your bodies are. It can be very powerful!

The most important thing to remember when lovemaking is that ORGASM IS NEVER THE GOAL! This does not mean that orgasm should not happen, of course. But the goal in lovemaking is to MERGE into ONE and thus experience Divine Communion. Orgasm is a pleasant side effect and can be an amazing climax. But if you focus on it as the goal, then you will miss everything else wonderful that can happen on the way there.

Furthermore, a man should NEVER orgasm before his partner is fully pleased. As we all know, a man gets heated up and aroused much quicker than a woman, which is why he orgasms sooner. Generally, around the time the man has orgasmed, the woman is just starting to get heated up. This is why it is crucial not to let your water "boil over" until she catches up to you.

Many things can be done in order to avoid this. Foreplay is crucial for heating a woman up. If you are using foreplay to arouse your Beloved, it should never be shorter than 30 minutes. And, if done correctly, it can last for hours.

Try giving her a sensual massage with heated oil. A sensual massage should not be too soft and relaxing, or you will put her to sleep. And yet it is not meant to be deep and painful either. The strokes should be long, slightly firm and sensual. You are looking to arouse your partner; so be sure to focus on her erogenous zones, but don't limit the massage to them. You can also perform manual or oral pleasure which, if done correctly, can be an art form unto itself. My favorite kind of foreplay is all of the above combined!!! There is something to be said about contrast and variety. And don't forget, foreplay should be mutual—you do it for her, and she does it for you. Ideally, take this approach with every aspect of your lovemaking, so that everything you do is a give and take, back and forth, an exchange of energy between two Divine and equal spiritual beings.

When you are through and both basking in the deep love you have shared for each other, be sure to ceremoniously dress one another (if you choose to put your clothes back on at all). Never let the other person put their own clothing back on by themselves. Once you're both dressed, gaze one last time into each other's eyes and thank them for allowing you to worship and to MERGE with them. There is no need to separate. Even as you physically walk away and carry on with your day, your spirits can still remain merged together in Love and Divine Union.

Elaine Caban, from Ft. Lauderdale, Florida, practices what she refers to as Tantric Therapy. After working for years as a Spiritual Healer, Counselor and Angel Intuitive, she now integrates Tantra into her work for therapeutic and healing purposes. She also performs various Tantric Ceremonies and Sacred Rituals for men, women and couples. You can learn more about Tantric Therapy at her website: Tantrictherapy.org

Awakening the Jesus and Mary Within

By Gabriella Hartwell

We were not created to possess, but to "be with."
~Gospel of Mary Magdalene

This is an amazing time we are living in right now. We are moving from the old way of relating and interacting in relationships to the new way of *being* in love, as we *be* with another person whom we choose to be in relationship with. What I mean is that no longer are we just choosing to physically share our selves, our time, our energy with another. We are being called to operate and be in the space, the vibration of love. Then we come together with another who is also *being*, just being as they are, IN the vibration, the frequency of love. There is a whole different energy around this than you may have previously experienced in relationships.

If you are reading this, then your consciousness, your intuition has already been knocking on your door, whispering: "Wait a minute, wait a minute, something is shifting here. This is not right for me anymore. The way that I have been acting, the way that I have been in relationship, what I have been accepting, what I have felt was acceptable is no longer working, because it doesn't ring true for me now."

I am a Relationship Life Coach and author of the book, *You Find Your Soul Mate When You Let Go of Searching*. As you may know, we have had a "fast food society", a fast food world, in that when we want something, we want it right away, whether it be food or a relationship. We have fast food restaurants and drive-thrus. We have dating websites where, if you want a date tonight, you go on a dating site and get it. We have had that mentality for so long in our modern world that it has just become habit. But we are moving now towards going within, and making ourselves whole FIRST, so that we can then experience *outside* of us that which reflects what is already *inside* of us. This will lead to a much deeper, more balanced relationship with another spiritual being in human form.

The thing to get to here is that you are complete *exactly* as you are. There is nothing you need outside of yourself to be happy or to be complete. Your happiness is a perspective. It is something you choose to feel and then, when you come together with another, you are sharing your *being* in love with them. As you are vibrating in this space of love within, and then being with another who is also in that space, you are both in love together. This is quite a different reality from seeking out a relationship simply to avoid being lonely.

Also, this is why I don't usually promote dating sites and dating in general, because of the importance of not searching. The whole energy of searching is not conducive to being within the flow of divine guidance as you walk through all of the moments of your life's journey. If you are searching for something, then you are saying to the universe: "I do not have this. I am lacking something. I do not have happiness so I am going outside of myself to try and find it. I do not have love so I am going outside of myself to find it."

I do promote going to singles groups or other groups or events where people are doing things that you enjoy and have in common with you, such as being single. The focus is not to find someone to go on a date with or even to necessarily romantically connect with someone. The purpose is to go and enjoy what you like to do, something you are interested in doing with others who are also interested in the same things. And then, if there's a connection made in the process, great. But there isn't that energy of expectation or lack attached to your approach.

If you let go of searching, then you come to the space of

feeling that it is okay to be on your own, to spend time on your own, to know that you don't need someone outside of you to be happy. MEN: you are being called *now* to go within and be connected to the woman inside of you, to the female essence and energy inside of you. WOMEN: You are being called *now* to go within and be connected to the man, the male energy inside of you. We are all being called to balance our male and female energies within ourselves so that we can then draw to us that form, that female or male physical form of another outside of us, to share our energies with.

When we balance these energies within, we come to the place of knowing and feeling that we are already complete. There is a widespread cultural agreement, expressed in a million different ways, that men are a certain way, and women are a certain way. If we believe that, then our behaviors will reflect that. Our relationships will be an extension of the roles that we, as men or women, have soaked up from society.

Ultimately, what we desire is a relationship with another that creates a loving space in which we are receiving love and giving love equally. But if we are stuck in these stale patterns of how men are supposed to be, and how women are supposed to be, then already there is no equality there. We are creating separation before we even begin. It isn't possible to create a relationship of real union within a constricted view of male and female energies.

What we are being called to do now is to *release* the ideas and perceptions of separation. By releasing these ideas and perceptions, we change the whole energy that we feel around relationships, around the opposite sex and even around ourselves. If you are a man and you feel that men are a certain way and that's just the way it is, then you're sending this energy to the female who is going to be in relationship with you; "I am like this, and you are supposed to be like this." Relationships are not black and white. You need to release this idea to open up to a new way of relating. To do that, you must go within and embrace the opposite sex energy within you.

We are being called to be more self-aware: to be aware of ourselves as we are in relationship with another, to be aware of the other as we are in relationship with them, without taking anything personally. When something challenging comes up within us while in a relationship, review it and take a good look at it. Relationships are meant to offer us some challenges, to offer us bumps along our journey. Why? Because we grow that way. If we didn't have these challenges, we wouldn't be able to grow. When you are having problems in your relationship, take a moment to be thankful that you have an opportunity to see something reflected back to you for you to receive, and to learn from. What is it? What's really going on? How can you take this experience within your relationship and use it as an opportunity for transformation?

I titled this essay *Awakening the Jesus and Mary Within*. Whatever religion you belong to doesn't matter. Let's simply look at Jesus and Mary as both being spiritual figures who we can use as examples, like characters in a book or players in a movie. Jesus was loving. He was an example of breaking down the barriers, all barriers created from separation: tax collectors and common people, Romans and Jews, women and men.

I'd like to take a closer look at the latter, the separation between men and women. There were many barriers of separation that he gave insight to and helped to transform, release and transition out of. He stated many times and showed in many ways that women are not less than men. They are equal and they can share in equal ways. The man needs the woman as the woman needs the man. We need each other to understand all aspects of ourselves, because within the man, there are womanly qualities and within the woman, there are manly qualities. When we acknowledge this and embrace this, we say yes to union, and no more separation. This is when we can actually have heaven on

Earth in our relationships. This is what we are being called to do. This is what we are moving into, fully NOW.

Jesus spoke with Mary Magdalene and connected in some deeper way with Mary. They had a very special relationship, whether or not you believe they were married. Mary, being accepting of Jesus and his teachings, such as how he presented men and women, was also open to breaking down the barriers of separation, to be in union, to be in unconditional love with herself, Jesus and with everyone. They had their own energies, their own individual essence and ray of light. But when they came together, their energies complemented each other. They had balanced the male, the female within themselves, the false perception around men and women, and had let go of separation to choose union. They came together and created Oneness.

I'd like to mention the number 11 here. Because we are in the 11th year, and moving forward we will be taking these 11th year insights with us, so to speak, into the years past 2011. So take the number 11. You have a 1 and a 1, both of which can exist separately. They are complete on their own. They are happy on their own. They can *be* on their own. But when 1 and 1 choose to come together, they create 11, which is an extension of their own being, of their inherent oneness. They come together to share their union.

We are being called now to embody UNION in all ways. I want to emphasis this word because it is so powerful. UNION. It's all contained in that word. **Un I on(e)**: *You and I are one*. **U n I on**: *You and I on a mission*. This is what we are doing now. We are coming together, complete in ourselves, while recognizing and acknowledging that we are One. As we do that, we make the choice to merge in action and become one together. Both of our physical bodies coming together to be one, one essence extending into each other by *being* together.

And as we come together, we then share this beingness with the rest of the world. We share this love with the rest of the world, however we choose to do so. In so doing, we find ourselves on a mission to serve humanity, to raise the vibration of love on this planet right now. We are awakening the Jesus and the Mary within us, so that we can let go of separation and enter fully into Union. We don't need to search for anything outside of ourselves. We don't need to feel that we need anyone outside of ourselves to be complete or happy. Jesus said that "The kingdom of God is within you". And God is love, so love is within you. It's connecting to that love within you which you then attract to yourself in another *being* who is also connecting with that same love within themselves. You are then ***being*** in love together. You find yourselves in Oneness together, on a mission to share that love with each other and with the rest of the world, anybody who comes in contact with you.

This is a powerful time. What an amazing opportunity for our souls to have chosen to be here now. We have a gift, that potential of finding love within. When we acknowledge it, then the next step is to take that knowingness forward to *be* in relationship with ourselves and with another in oneness, in union. All it takes is awakening the Jesus and Mary energy within us, connecting to the male and the female essence that we all can access, releasing all barriers of separation. Separation truly is just an illusion. It takes merely a shift of perception and a reconnection to ourselves to change things around and enter that kingdom within. Welcome to heaven ***right now*** here on Earth. It starts with each one of us.

Gabriella Hartwell lives on the island of Kauai, Hawaii, is an Intuitive Relationship Life Coach, mentor, and author of the book *You Find Your Soul Mate When You Let Go of Searching*. She offers coaching sessions for singles and couples as well as angel readings and dream interpretations. Visit her website at: www.EmergingSoul.com.

To the Man, Lover, Life Partner, Friend

By Sarah Nolan

I write this vulnerable, raw and exposed letter as a gift to you; a view of the essence of the woman I am, what I want, what I desire and a few notes I feel may be helpful for you to hear in order to prepare for a deeper love.

A woman such as me wants a man with a soulful leaning, an instinctual nature, an endurance that will enable you to identify, understand and embrace my deepest substance, my very being. This takes great courage and strength of mind, stuff of which fairytales and stories of past generations are made of: the noble hero, the great knight slaying the dragon or the demon at the gates of the castle of the woman he loves. Not that I require a great knight to slay my demons. I myself have faced them alone. But I need to know that you are indeed willing to face your own demons first, to experience the joining with me.

You will need the courage and strength I speak of, for you must allow my substance, my exposed being to wash over you, wash over your shield, your armor, your barriers, your preconceived ideas and expectations. This will challenge you, I will challenge you. I will stand in front of you, real and exposed, and test your every belief surrounding how I should be, how I should behave, look, speak, fuck, think. I want you to stand up to this challenge with an open mind, with quiet strength and dignity. I will not tolerate it if you run, control or manipulate. I must see you stand tall, be a safe and stable port. This is to prove to me that you are willing to weather the storm that my femininity at times harbors in order to get to the tranquil waters of its basic existence.

You may find yourself aroused by this challenge. You may be

shocked, amazed, scared, or feeling as vulnerable and frightened as I am right now. Or you may find that you will be empowered. Whatever it is you experience I need you to feel it, you need to feel it, embrace it, own it, live it and allow me to be part of it. Don't worry about how I may react or cope, believe me. For as soft as my appearance may be, there is nothing that may come up throughout this process that will deter me. My love and my commitment once given to you is unconditional, and my strength immense.

No criticisms please, my body is my gift to you as yours is to me. She is sacred, she is my temple, she has served me well all these years, experiencing the wonder, playfulness and pleasure of ecstasy and orgasm, the physical pain and elation of childbirth, the torment and grief of rejection that physically manifested as heartache while I cried myself to sleep at night when a love affair had ended. I adore her every curve, blemish and her exquisite receptivity. She has provided me the physical and mental agility I've needed to fight my battles and make my way through this life, forge my own identity, my own career, my own path.

It has taken me a long time to reclaim her unique beauty, softness and wonder, taken time to fall in love with the battle scars I now carry with pride. And it has taken even more time still to reclaim the trust I have needed to re-discover how to be strong enough to invite you in. The trust may have been there all the time. But somehow I had hidden it along the way, allowing fear to shield me from any potential vulnerability and danger. I had to believe that I would find the trust when the right man appeared. And with that knowledge you need to remember that, always, and treat my trust with the sacred respect it deserves.

My Divine Feminine nature, something I have fought for in a society where its very presence is disregarded, is in fact one of your greatest allies. Worship her, value her, learn from her and your masculinity will soar. Follow the shape, scent and subtle cues of her intricate knowledge and movement. Then alongside me learn the story of how a deep sensual and loving connection will take you to a level that no other external force can. Once this is obtained I can guarantee you will no longer hunger for power, material objects and hostility to feel in possession of your masculinity. Your masculinity will then flow naturally through you. And being able to watch and partake within this process, my femininity will soar alongside you. For without one another, neither of us are truly complete and whole.

Take your time with this process, so that the knowledge learned is interwoven in your subconscious. Become enlightened and present around me; be attentive, supportive and kind. From that place you will quickly see that it is you also who will benefit. Remember that I love you, I desire you and I want you. I accept you as you are and I do not wish to change a thing about you. You are enough, and I will support you and stand beside you as an equal. What I ask of you is to provide a safe and sacred space where I am, without judgment or fear, able to be myself. No boundaries, no controls, no violence, no deceit or games; just space for me to simply be, and where you also can become as open and exposed as I will be.

Love me as I am, be present with me, and then you will discover you will instinctively find your way around my heart, body and soul. With this pure intention of yours in place, I will be able to commit in a way such that together we can create a depth of union that will surpass anything either of us has experienced before.

I understand this task is an enormous undertaking; the duality of such a deep and heartfelt connection is a double-edged sword. There is the strong existence of risk and fear. I also acknowledge and feel the painful reality that this growth can bring up; leaving you feeling raw and exposed, lacking that protective armor. But I will do everything in my power to make this process as painless as possible. If you can find it in your heart and soul to give me that which I desire, then I will give you everything in return… I will surrender.

Sarah Nolan, from Queensland, Australia, has worked previously in women's health and well-being and is passionate about the empowerment of women and their true higher selves and how this heightens the connection between the masculine and feminine. She is currently in the process of working on her first book.

Using Sex Magic to Manifest Our Heart's Desires

By Barbara Yednak

Sex and spirituality are two areas of my life in which I seem to be in complete balance. I am a free-spirited individual who lives from my heart. I am currently 59 years young and enjoying my life to the fullest, while manifesting life with my creator. My journey began to shift at an accelerated speed when I decided to get a divorce after a 36-year marriage. During this divorce process I began to consciously manifest, and at the same time I started to meditate on a daily basis. I knew about the transference of energy through thought and because I am a massage therapist and also work as a healing energy channel, I already knew how powerful this energy can be.

I decided to delve a bit deeper into energy, and to experiment with sexual energy in particular in a few different ways. I learned that sexual energy is one of the most powerful energies available to us, and easily accessible, but not easily or often talked about. I have no problem discussing this subject. But many women seem to shy away from this type of conversation. What tends to open up the lines of communication is when I begin to tell women that I have used sexual energy to achieve many things that I now have in my life.

In the past four years I have gone through an amicable divorce; I built/contracted a 2,800 square foot home that is free and clear, no mortgage; I have a great lover; I have asked for landscape pavers, and I received them; I found a source of income in which I didn't have to go out and get a job unless I wanted to… and so many other things I have asked for have shown up.

Much of this has been accomplished through the use of sexual energy. Some refer to this as sex magic. To me, there is no magic. It is all about intention and the power of thought. This can be done through the actual sexual act, by sending out your intention during an orgasm, whether that is done with another individual, through solitary sex or through the use of pictures such as a Sigil or Sacred Yoni art.

When I first began using this sexual energy, I was by myself. In the moment that I was about to experience the ecstasy of that release (orgasm) I would shout out and visualize what I wanted. I would try to be very specific, and often I would write out what I wanted and memorize it clearly so that I wouldn't leave anything out. One of the first times I did this, I asked for a tall man, who was responsible and financially stable, healthy, who would have great body parts and would know how to use those parts. I did this in April. By the end of May, this man showed up in my life. He plays tennis and has all of the characteristics that I'd requested. He would also turn out to be the answer to many of my manifestations. When I met this man, I didn't know that he was going to be such an important part of my life. He still is.

A warning, however: you need to be very specific when putting in a request to the Universe. I know someone who asked for a soft-hearted, cuddly, loyal and loving male with big brown eyes, etc. —and ended up with a great dog who fit everything she asked for! It took her a while to figure out that she got exactly what she'd asked for, but was not specific enough. I also know a man who had a list of attributes on his bathroom mirror of all the things he wanted in a woman. But he failed to mention the word "healthy" in his list. He did find a woman with many of those characteristics, but found out soon after they began dating that she had herpes. Again, BE VERY SPECIFIC!

As I continued to consciously manifest, I used other tools like a vision board, and I believe this all helped with the process. I remember looking online for a house for myself that would have a casita attached, so that I could have extra income if I wanted one. I indeed found it, and put the floor plan on the wall next to my bed so that the first thing I saw when I opened my eyes in the morning was the picture of the home I was going to own, free and clear. I placed all of the furniture in the house where it was going to be and I also put out the intent that I wanted anyone who walked into this home to feel the love inside and out. My home is currently referred to as HeartSpace. I have had full moon/gong ceremonies, fireside talks and channeling sessions, and people constantly tell me that they can feel the love in my home. This is exactly what I had asked for.

Some other methods for manifesting through sex are the use of a Sigil, a symbol created for a specific magical purpose. A Sigil is usually made up of a complex combination of several specific figures or pictures, each with a specific meaning or intent. This can be created very easily. What you would do is write down your intent in the center of a sheet of paper at least 8.5 x 11 inches, and around your intent place sexual pictures that are arousing to you. Use your own pictures that you may have taken, or pictures that you have found in magazines or online and place them around the intent. During the day, find some quiet time and just look at this sheet of paper. You don't even need to read the intent but you DO need to feel those sexual feelings that the pictures you have chosen should bring to you. Try to use as many of your senses as possible while doing this.

Another form of manifesting through sex is to sit quietly in a meditative state and think about a time when you had great sex. Take yourself mentally back to that place and experience it again, as if it was happening over and over again. Think of the smells, the sounds, using as many of your senses as possible, taking yourself back to that orgasm you experienced, and put out your intent to the universe. Use your imagination. It is your tool to create.

One of my recent methods that I have chosen to work with is something that I call Sacred Yoni Art. *Yoni*, the Sanskrit word for "divine passage" (the vagina), also means "sacred space". It is clearly recognized by the ancients as the seat of sexual power. I believe women need to celebrate the many faces of the feminine and be proud of their sacred space. This form of art that I create is creatively personalized, and can be proudly exhibited as a reminder of your own source of power. What I have done is taken a photo of my own yoni and placed it in art. For example, I have a picture of a large Buddha head on my wall and I've placed a large amaryllis flower in front of that Buddha. I then placed a picture of my own yoni in the flower. No one would ever see this unless they were looking closely for it. I would use this picture as a way of honoring myself, and the power that I have within me. I can see myself as a beautiful piece of art, and as I admire and love myself, I also am asking my creator to honor my intent. When you are in total joy, manifesting is very easy.

This yoni artwork began because I was a little disturbed by the fact that women did not like their own sacred space, and were choosing plastic surgery to change their appearance. I want women (and men) to celebrate the many faces of the feminine yoni and to Honor Thyself. Men can help by understanding that women have many shapes and sizes, just as men do, and that their personal preferences have to do with their own beliefs that they have chosen to accept. We all have our own likes or dislikes. We should never impose our beliefs or expectations on others. They are limiting and if expressed, can be hurtful to others, whether male or female.

Since this book is to help men deepen their relationships with women, I need to state that ALL of the methods that I've mentioned here can also be used by men to achieve their hearts desires. I have combined the yoni (female) and the *lingam* (male part) in artwork together in my manifesting.

Partners in a relationship can also use many of the methods stated above. There is much to be said for the power of multiple energies combining, to achieve great desires in this lifetime. The scientist and visionary, Gregg Braden, has stated that all it takes is the square root of one percent of the population gathered together with the same intention to make a shift in the consciousness of humanity. This is only about 8,000 people. If there are two loving individuals in a state of pure love, gratitude and joy, who release their intentions together at the time of the orgasm, the likelihood of these intentions manifesting into their desires is greatly enhanced.

I have used all of these methods to manifest the things mentioned above into my life, but I want you to know that this power is limitless. I have also used this for anti-aging, to remain healthy and to keep myself in a place of love and joy. I believe that Source, Spirit, God, Goddess—whatever you choose to label it—gave each of us a gift. And this "gift" is pure love. It begins by Loving Thyself.

My loving wish for everyone is to use this sexual energy wisely. It is the most powerful energy for manifesting ALL of your heart's desires.

Barbara Yednak, from Phoenix, Arizona, is a licensed massage therapist as well as a healing energy channel. She enjoys photography and graphic art and designed the cover art for a recently published book, *The Light Upon My Path*. She is also part of a band called the Desert Winds Steel Orchestra. To watch and enjoy the music go to: www.youtube.com/watch_popup?v=YKWCsY1Da28. You can find Barbara on Facebook at: www.facebook.com/byednak or: www.facebook.com/pages/HeartSpace-Community/136518193082775?ref=ts. For your own personalized Sacred Yoni and/or Lingam art to use in sex magic for manifesting what you desire, contact Barbara at: azhealer@mindspring.com, or go to Yonifaces on Facebook for more information and designs: www.facebook.com/profile.php?id=100002002686734&ref=ts#!/profile.php?id=100002002686734&sk=info

Master's Muse

A story by Kathleen Ann Staley

(This was previously published in her book "Spirit Children", published by Publishamerica.)

Verona, Italy, A.D. 1490

At morning light, Verona sparkled with a magical glow. Sixteen-year-old Victor rushed to the cathedral to say his daily prayers. It was his fondest wish to learn how to sculpt marble in the style of the Italian Masters. He prayed and prayed for the talent and strength to transform stone into magnificent works of art. He believed the spirit of the stone determined the shape that it becomes.

Victor attended classes taught by one of the priests. Father Paul was a very skilled artist, but his work lacked style. According to the church, male forms were Godlike. Artists were not allowed to paint or sculpt the nude female form, however, because it was considered sinful and was forbidden. Male models instead wore the clothing of females and posed for the sketching sessions. Only the male anatomy was studied in the morgues. Dead bodies were dissected and illustrated in great detail. Women were not allowed to become artists or to pose as models.

Victor desired to sketch from a real-life female model. He had great respect for the female form, and was known as a womanizer. His passion for women had caused many problems for him in his strict and structured life. In his spare time, Victor studied Greek and Roman mythology. The legends of Goddesses, Sirens and Mermaids intrigued him. He fantasized about Athena and Aphrodite, and had daydreams about most beautiful women.

He'd read the story of a beautiful maiden, Medusa, who was turned into an awful creature called a Gorgon. The hideous creature had snakes growing from its head with poison blood. Medusa offended the Goddesses for seducing Zeus in the Temple of Athena. One look at a Gorgon turned a man to stone. The tale of Medusa frightened him and helped him to avoid angering any deity.

Victor tried to devote himself to the church, but his passion for women kept him from becoming a priest. Night after night, he dreamed about Adam and Eve, the Garden of Eden and the story of the forbidden fruit. His lust motivated his desire.

On the way to the cathedral one day, Victor saw the most beautiful woman he had ever seen, being escorted to Mass. He stopped in his tracks and nearly fell to the ground when their eyes met. Her hair was the color of spun gold. She had pure white skin, large, sad blue eyes and a small rosy mouth. She was dressed as a noble woman.

Victor imagined that she was the Goddess of Love, sent to him from heaven. He followed and watched her. He was so distracted by his lust that he forgot to go to his studio class that day. At the end of Mass, the woman vanished in the crowd. Victor desperately looked for her and asked everyone he knew who she was. The obsession disturbed him, and he was unable to focus on anything else. He wrote lengthy poems on the virtues of women, and romantic verses about the elusive, golden-haired angel.

After several weeks, Victor discovered the woman's name was Catherine de Medici, a noble from the Court of Verona. She was the epitome of elegance and grace. Catherine was already promised in marriage to a Count from Spain. She was untouched by men and was virtuous, to a fault. Her attendants were the only people allowed to touch her fair, ivory skin and floor-length, golden hair.

Victor continued to obsess over Catherine and lusted for her day and night. He sketched her image on all of his tablets and envisioned her nude, posing for a painting or a marble sculpture. Victor studied the other marble sculptures, done by Michelangelo and Rafael and compared them to muscular men. He believed that none of the artists of the time had captured the true loveliness of the female form.

The priests taught the students of art that the female, Eve, was the basis for all Sin of Adam and all Humanity. It was forbidden to look upon the nude female form, so they studied male anatomy. The priests also insisted upon covering all genitalia in the artworks. If an artist working in the church was led into the temptation to use a real-live female model, they would be excommunicated and damned by the Pope.

Victor despised having to conform to the standards of the church. He was a free-spirited, youthful visionary, who believed he was meant to be the greatest sculptor of all time. He constantly boasted about his superior talent, and tended to ridicule his peers. Although he had not actually finished any of his projects in class, he pretended to be working on a secret piece that would be the most impressive creation ever completed, to present to the Pope.

One day, his teacher asked to see the project he was working on. Victor refused to let anyone see it. He was ashamed that he had lied to everyone; but continued the charade. He asked the teacher to wait until he was finished and then he would present the project, soon. He worked day and night on a slab of white Italian marble, chiseling and sanding the dense stone. Victor was unable to focus on his work and continued to fantasize about Catherine de Medici.

He left his studio to get a loaf of bread and a bottle of wine. Along the way, he noticed a carriage, led by a white stallion, tethered to a post. His heart pounded and his face became flushed when he saw his beloved Goddess, Catherine within. She was alone.

Victor approached the carriage carefully, and introduced himself. She was very pleasant and held out her hand. When Victor reached for her hand, she pulled it away and said, "You must not touch me. But it is a pleasure to meet you."

Victor blushed with embarrassment. "I meant no offense, dear lady", he said. "I only wanted to see your lovely face, up close. I have admired you from afar, for many months."

Catherine was flattered by the attention, but stopped smiling when her father returned to the carriage. Victor quickly handed her one of his love poems, and told her where his studio was. He then asked her to be a model for his masterpiece. But she did not answer. Victor was aware of Catherine's engagement, but didn't care. He was determined to have her, no matter the cost. Every fiber of his being was aching with desire for his Goddess of Love. All that night, he dreamed about making love with her at the foot of a statue of Athena. He woke up in a cold sweat when he remembered what happened to Medusa when she defiled Athena's temple. He was relieved that it was only a dream.

The next morning, Victor began to sculpt the final shapes of his masterpiece. He was inspired by Catherine and her loveliness. The teacher and fellow students were anxious to see what Victor was working on, and had difficulty honoring his privacy. They stayed away though, awaiting the completion. All of the others finished their projects; but nonetheless, they weren't as talented as Victor.

He worked through the day and into the evening. His solitude was interrupted suddenly by a knock at the door. To Victor's delight, Catherine had come to visit him. She offered to pose for him—in the nude. Victor was so excited he could barely contain himself. She removed her gown and revealed her exquisite, luminous body. Victor was practically drooling when the cloth fell from her small breasts.

Catherine said to him: "Whatever you do, do not touch me, or there will be dire consequences!" Victor assumed that she was referring to the wrath of her father.

He worked on various sketches and eventually applied his tools to the stone. During the process, Victor's heart was still pounding, and he felt as though he was on fire with desire.

Every time he looked at her, the feeling of lust overwhelmed him. He worked for a few hours, while Catherine posed, barely moving a muscle. When Victor began to chisel the upper torso and head, he was unable to control himself. He threw down his tools, rushed into Catherine's arms, and they made passionate love.

In the aftermath of their passion, Victor screamed in horror as he gazed upon what had become the hideous face of the Medusa. Snakes twisted out of Catherine's head, and her eyes became fire-red. She wrapped her dragon-like body around Victor, and squeezed the life from him. Both of their bodies merged together, into solid stone.

In the morning, the teacher and the rest of the class arrived to see Victor's masterpiece. In the corner of the studio was an exquisite marble sculpture of entwined lovers. It was the best work from the class, worthy of a true Italian Master. Victor was never seen again. And all images of Catherine had mysteriously vanished.

Kathleen Ann Staley, from Paradise, California, has deep passion for art and humanity. She writes positive stories about love, hope and world peace. She has six volumes of short stories to date, from Publishamerica. Her fondest desires are to have movies made from her stories, and to travel the world. She plans to continue writing from her heart and soul for the rest of her life. You can contact her at: skittyclark@aol.com, or join her on Facebook at: www.facebook.com/profile.php?id=1679290454

I See Love

By Jena Greer

Since I was a teen, I would write poems about a love that I once knew. It baffled me how personal they were—as though it had been a real experience—because I hadn't actually had a relationship yet. Over the years I wrote it off as an overly romantic tendency. But I have finally come to terms with the truth. This imaginary idea that affected me as if it were a memory, was in fact a deep desire to connect, to be in union as are yin and yang. Each part is perfect in and of itself; but combined together they become truly powerful, like the ebb and flow of the tides. Intertwined with each other, they manifest and create life.

Maybe I had this soul-filled love in another life. But I don't think that's what generated the desire inside me at such a young age. Instead, I believe it was something that is an innate desire inside of all of us. We long to love and be loved and belong. However much I have tried to complicate this fact over the years, the simple truth remains, beyond fear and ego. I too want to love and be loved; yet I'll stay by myself until I really know that the right kind of person has come into my life.

The experience of love must meet a standard in my eyes. Many say not to have expectations. Yet it is healthy, even essential to not settle for less than we desire. For me, it isn't that I have expectations of how I think *he* should be—but of how *we* should be together. I feel and believe it is possible to really connect and bond with someone in an esoteric way, and I refuse to give my heart and soul for anything less again.

I want to have faith again, to trust and feel vulnerable and be excited about love. I want to know that I didn't settle for someone *close* to what I want; but that I waited until it was *right,* and we both know that what we have together is rare and precious and not to be taken for granted.

When we are lonely, we cling to something that is familiar and comfortable. With comfort comes laziness most often. With laziness comes carelessness and demise of the relationship. If we set our standards high, of ourselves and of others, keeping in mind a goal or a dream of things being the best they can be, then we stay on our best behavior through most anything. We plan and care and cherish what we hold in high regard, although it isn't the most comfortable at times. For me, it should be exciting and challenging and worthy of my attention.

I am by no means saying that the arms of your loved one shouldn't feel like the safest place on earth. I am saying it *is* the most precious place possible, and we must choose wisely. I am aware that this is difficult. We have habits and comfort zones we must walk away from so that we can then allow something wonderful into our experience. I am prepared to break free from old ways that no longer serve me, to make room for something wonderful that will.

I have noticed how many people have no idea how to make love. I hear women speak about sex like it's the equivalent of a pedicure. When the bond of two people is deep, the passion will be as well. I'm talking about groundbreaking, unbridled passion that forever links you with your lover. I am NOT talking about sex. Sex is animalistic and if you feel you need that, then you have taken up with the wrong partner. Having sex is another instant gratification experience that has no bearing on your life, no food for your soul. Sex is a soulless act that comes from filling holes (quite literally). Anytime you are filling a void, you are not fulfilling your highest potential; nor are you manifesting the highest potential mate into your life experience.

I believe that relationships are a lot of work; but work in terms of *creating a masterpiece*—something that will be witnessed by others, and then they too will want what you have created, for themselves. If we stop settling and step out of our comfort zones and reach for the highest possibility, we don't just satisfy ourselves, we in turn raise the bar for humanity. A ripple effect starts in honesty and integrity, works its way passionately through our bedrooms, sits heartily in our family and game rooms, tends our garden and feeds the thoughts and desires of mankind. We are a collective consciousness; we need to own up to that responsibility. It has to start somewhere. Why not by engaging and dancing in life with someone you truly love and trust?

A sign of truth that you're in a real relationship: if it is the real deal, then the other person **will** feel the same about you. If not, then you are under a delusion and it is none of what I seek or speak of. A relationship is two-sided. If you are told "no", be an adult and respect the fact that you will experience even better than what you thought you would have with the person that doesn't return the same feelings for you that you. Let go, and **allow** yourself to be open to the right person, who feels just as strongly about you. Equality is a must.

I wonder if there was a time when relationships were not consumed by issues of neglect, codependency, abuse and infidelity. I wonder when people stopped caring, stopped trusting. What started the need for us to justify settling for less of others and ourselves? I see a love that to others seems unrealistic. And if I hadn't tried time and again to settle for less, I might still agree that high standards should be lowered. Since I have tried and always felt more of a lack with a partner than I did by myself, I have realized that it isn't worth it to settle and be left wanting. I now understand that *settling* is the fuel to this empty cycle that most of us have suffered from.

I see love as hard work, in terms of maintaining that higher standard, creating that masterpiece. When we share our love with another, it is our sole responsibility to keep ourselves in check, to be accountable for each decision we make that directly affects those we love. We all need to remember that we are each here to have an individual life experience and that even though we are choosing to share that experience with another, there is no room for ownership, control or insecurity. There are boundaries not to be crossed. Like our best friends, we accept each other's different lives and choices. So why do otherwise with our love partner? This is most important to me.

Previously in my life, I may not have been capable of loving the way I imagined it should be. But I feel that I am close to ready, close to treating another just as I would have him treat me. I wonder how we can bring real love back to fruition, back to reality, back to union? How many of us are willing to blindly trust again, yet simultaneously maintain our sense of self, so that we no longer lose ourselves in relationships and put ourselves in a position of inequality, one way or the other?

I used to try and convince myself that my soul mate was an alien, because I couldn't imagine him to be like anyone I had ever met. But now that I have grown in love, I am surrounded by people with qualities I would love to emulate, and I believe that someday soon I will attract the kind of person that I can share true love with.

I see love differently now. It isn't something to fill a void with; which is the impetus for our own journey of finding peace within ourselves. I believe we must first be balanced as an individual before we attempt to be whole as a couple. Only then, can we achieve a healthy and fulfilling union.

I see love as something that doesn't fade, something that doesn't lie, unless, perhaps, it's postponing a surprise =). I see love in a sense that our souls could meet up between each lifetime and laugh and cry and share openly all the experiences we had without any shame, judgment or insecurity. And since we are always the same souls, no matter what life we are living, I see that love can honestly be shared the same way during our physical lifetimes.

This is what I seek. And now that I am aware, I am capable, and am not in search of filling a void. I am attracting like-minded people. And I know that, as for the one I seek, we will both know when we have found each other. I know that I will see love again when it is true; when I am ready to give myself and to receive him fully. Until then, I have plenty of self-growth to do, and I am in no rush. In fact, as I see love, time is irrelevant; time is linear and does not exist in a collective infinite consciousness or in the union of two universal souls.

I see love as though I am a Goddess, and he will be my match, my equal. Our differences will add to our lives and broaden our experiences, both separate and together. I see love as a gift, one that should be shared, given both care and effort each day. I see love as a constant reminder to both of us of what we have, and what we do not wish to give up.

Jena Greer, aka Jenasis Free, from Santa Fe, New Mexico is a published poet, philanthropist, philosopher and writer of the movie 2012: The Collective. She lives to CoExist & Assist without exclusion. She is also the founder of Namaste Journey—Etheric Artist (recreating your OBE's and Experiences into tangible work) and KIND: Kindred Inclination for Namastic Development Philanthropy—Ascension Philosophy. Namaste.

The Erotic Way: Heeding the Call

By Tantrica Maya

I have been a single woman since my divorce in 1986. Chronologically, I am fifty years old. Creatively speaking, I am ageless. I have enjoyed sexual relationships with men that number in the hundreds. Some of them have been as short as ten minutes: like when I met a man while browsing books in a well known bookstore. We felt this sudden, strong attraction, turned to one another and, like magnets, our lips were drawn together. It was a magical moment.

Many others have consisted of an evening out to dinner, followed by being together to satisfy mutual needs. Brief and intense encounters became especially plentiful when I ventured into "touch therapy" as a profession. Now, I feel very fortunate to be sharing my recent years, and hopefully many future ones, with a partner that I am destined to travel with together on further erotic adventures.

In 2005 I left the conventional workforce of school teaching in order to pursue a new path that I thought would take me into the spa services arena. The Universe had other plans, however. Unbeknownst to me at the time, I was to go down a rugged road that along the way would invoke more wisdom to add to my spiritual insights. I would gather a new sexual awareness in the form of tantric teachings. In addition, I would receive the creative energy to fuse these into rewarding endeavors on many levels. I would keep an open mind and heart throughout this journey that would lead me both to a wealth of information—as well as an unpleasant law enforcement encounter.

My spa services business had evolved into the role of a courtesan. I simply wanted to have a lot of sex. And men were only too happy to oblige me. The fact that I would be given money to do so was just an incredibly perfect arrangement! Even the aforementioned legal encounter in the form of an undercover investigation, leading to an arrest for prostitution, did not deter me. I felt strongly that I had the right to receive money for the time and love that I was giving to others.

I understood that these activities could be associated with sex trafficking and drug abuse; but also that there are exceptions. And I was one of them. The law simply could not make room for those of us who enjoyed making a living in this gray area. This was a time of transition for me and my judgment was questionable. I made no attempt to stay "under the radar".

It was only when I met my beloved and our relationship began, that I started to feel more grounded and was ready to face the full extent of my reality. Two issues were paramount. One was that this lifestyle had serious ramifications unless I was vigilant about my health, my safety and steering clear of further legal actions. The second was that in all honesty, I was really doing this to satisfy my own sexual fantasies, and the lust that they generated.

Influenced by my budding relationship and my additional research into tantra, I began to feel a conviction to practice as a healer and keep my integrity intact. And for me, that meant serving humanity through a different prism of erotica. It had to be an approach that would not be based on my lust. It would not be focused on the genitals alone.

As time went on, I began to rein in my sexual boundaries. I omitted all sex acts except for lingam and prostate massages. Last April I experienced a spiritual epiphany, and realized that I would be a more effective teacher of tantra if I eliminated genital touch completely. I realized that by offering genital massage as a culminating act, I was actually encouraging the ego to get involved in the ritual.

The essence of tantra is to induce an erotic trance, so that the ego is quieted. Once the client has experienced the various states of arousal that arise from my ministrations—which include silk scarves, heated rocks and towels, and deliberate loving touch—they can absorb the experience by being still. A genital massage, instead, awakens them from this place and so the healing benefits are greatly reduced. Essentially, it brings forth the ego in a subtler form, which I believe is the antithesis of what a tantra healing experience is all about. It is for that reason that genital massage is not a part of my interpretation of a tantric healing ceremony.

When I share tantra with a visitor, I do so in a ritual that is heart-based. Arousal is encouraged and it is honored by connecting it visually to the heart. Through my creative interpretations of tantra, my seekers are transported to a place of timeless bliss. As they experience this connection, so do I. This is the act of making love happen. It is a simple ripple of affection devoted to the universe. It fosters serenity, peacefulness and a quiet state of being. In other words, it takes us out of the day-to-day struggle of the external reality. This outlook remains long after the ritual is over.

A client describes their experience of this state: "It's relinquishing the past and the future, quieting my mind, focusing on every sensation in the present moment, from each breath to each loving touch; allowing myself to reap the greatest pleasure from the simplest sensations; realizing that my entire body is a sexual organ. It is an awakening to the moment. It comes about when you are willing to receive pleasure without the distractions of yesterday and tomorrow. It is within the awareness that the Goddess energy of love is flowing over and through your entire body, that you enter a sense of timeless bliss. It is not a sexual encounter, but a fuller experience involving all of the senses. Instead of the senses becoming dull with relaxation, they become vivid, with each one overflowing through another until the entire body is vibrating on a new level—a higher state of being. That is how I experienced Maya's Sacred Healing Tantric Journey."

My experience in the encounter with this particular seeker was both extraordinary and typical. From the very start of the journey, consisting of breath work to slow down our minds, and visualization designed to open and expand our hearts and entire beings, we ignite the process of going within. From there, the seeker is led to my altar, a massage table illuminated from below with miniature strings of light. As I begin to stroke the person's body before me with love and tenderness, I continue to connect strongly with their divine presence which I can sense in my heart. It is immensely loving and gracious. It brings with it a force of energy that is shared with my seeker. It is joy. It is love. It is acceptance. It is forgiveness. It is appreciation. It is all of the feelings that the seeker expressed above. Why would they be any different? We have become one. We both experience a heightened sense of sexual arousal at various times during the journey. When the end of the journey is at hand, the seeker is shrouded in cotton linens so that he can absorb the healing at a cellular level. In this phase it becomes apparent that tantra is indeed a form of yoga and meditation. The benefits are cumulative and last longer than the journey itself.

Spicing Things Up

I enjoy expressing myself sexually in other ways besides neo-tantra. One of them is role-playing different scenarios that can connect me with enormous emotions. The archetypal darkness of a woman's essence, as depicted in society as the slut, can pack an emotional punch. My submissive side is expressed sexually when my partner speaks to me in street language while we're having sex. He is very aggressive and "subjects" me to spankings as well as "ordering me" with the use of explicit instructions on how I am to pleasure him. This turns me on immensely and, like a lioness, I am reduced to my primitive desires. I am obedient to my master. I have several other fantasies, such as an incest one, which he is only too happy to indulge me in.

When I see clients for role-play, also known as Dark Tantra, I switch. I am the dominant one, the dom. I give the orders. I play with clients under the guise of various powerful roles including the teacher, mother, aunt, executive, seductress or nurse. Sexual boundaries are maintained. There is no need for full sex acts in order for me to feel my power as a woman, and for a client to glory in it. This service would not be in such demand if their female partners could access this innate power. Until then, I am willing to offer them a sacred space to be humbled in such a way as to satisfy their deeper, primitive longings.

Recently my beloved and I began to discuss experiencing sex acts with others. To that end we plan to visit a swinger's club and seek out a new adventure. This discussion of bringing others into our relationship has only been possible because of the deep bond that we formed over the past three years. Had I attempted to broach this topic too soon in our relationship, it may have backfired and created a complicated situation. It may have exposed insecurities with a force that could have crushed what we were building. Doubts about my readiness for a commitment to another person might have become a looming question mark for both of us. By waiting until the foundation was strong, the topic was managed well. Building the foundation has been an ongoing deliberate process which we do not take lightly.

Like any other adult relationship in its infancy, we had to negotiate new emotional issues as they arose. We realized that romance is a priority. To keep it as such, we live separately. As we each maintain our own households we have less of the mundane to discuss. Although I might suggest a certain decorating idea, or he may carry my groceries up to my third floor condo, it is done on occasion and is not an expectation. As long as we are comfortable in each other's home, and know that we can rely on each other when needed, we feel content with our arrangement. It keeps the dynamic flowing in such a way that when we need to have a serious discussion, we can be fully present. We do not carry resentments about minor disagreements over how we spend our money, or who kept each other awake by tossing and turning on a previous night.

Having both been married, we truly understand how the myriad assortment of decisions that arise from sharing a home can become a burden to the romance of a relationship. Another reason that living separately works for us is because each of us has a strong desire to keep a certain amount of autonomy. We are not willing to risk creating a cycle by which we give so much priority to the relationship that we sabotage our self-esteem. Remaining together emotionally, but having physical boundaries, forces us to regularly show ourselves that we can each make it in this world alone. That perspective makes us appreciate how special we are, both to ourselves and to each other.

Revealing Her Essence

All women have the archetypal Goddess energy at their core. However, most women are not really aware of this power to heal themselves and others. There are many reasons they do not have this knowledge on a conscious level. The obvious one is what society does to a female's psyche from a very young age. In short, she is relentlessly bombarded with both hidden and overt messages to repress her very essence. She is taught about the world from a masculine perspective. She is taught to compete as opposed to cooperate, to analyze her thoughts as opposed to feeling them, to submit to the demands of others as opposed to remaining steadfast in her convictions. She must learn to adapt to the unconscious world where she feels like an outsider to her very being. She is confused about her body and how to relate to a man. She becomes buried alive.

The Divine Feminine nature is an endless reservoir of love and wisdom. But with whom and how much of this birthright should she share? Under what circumstances does she reveal a deeper, more exposed part of herself? Who is deserving of her generosity? Who can accept it without feeling threatened by such a tremendous overflowing source of desire and passion? She muddles through these thoughts and emotions without mentors or messages for navigating her birthright. She begins to abandon them. She tries, often in vain, to comprehend what society expects from her. Too often she never finds the key to unlock this mystery. She remains asleep to herself, to her chosen mate, and as a role model to any children they may have. Both endure the consequences of an unrealized birthright. For without the strength of a feminine compass, a man is unable to reach his own fuller potential as a human being.

Some men are beginning to recognize how the repression of women over the ages is affecting their well-being. They are acknowledging a sense of emptiness, and a longing for greater intimacy. They are searching for a sense of satisfaction in the only places that society has been telling them, subconsciously, that they might find that ultimate satisfaction: pornography, strip clubs, paid sexual encounters and complex affairs. As they delve deeper into these areas, they further distance themselves from any possibility of forming an intimate bond with their chosen mate.

The Awakening Male

Fortunately, men such as Arjuna Ardagh in his blog, "The Translucent View", have eloquently outlined the intricacies of the female essence and the very steps a man must take in order for it to be revealed. This is just a portion of his post entitled *Why It Is Wise to Worship a Woman*:

"…At the essence of every woman's heart is the Divine Feminine. It contains everything that has ever been beautiful, or lovely, or inspiring, in any woman, anywhere, at any time. The very essence of every woman's heart is the peak of wisdom, the peak of inspiration, the peak of sexual desirability, the peak of soothing, healing love. The peak of everything. But it's protected, for good reason, by a series of concentric walls. To move inwardly from one wall to the next requires that you intensify your capacity to devotion, and as you do so, you are rewarded with Grace. This is not something you can negotiate verbally with a woman. She doesn't even know consciously how to open those gates herself. They are opened magically and invisibly by the keys of worship.

"If you stand on the outside of the outermost wall, all you have available to you, like many other unfortunate men, is pornography. For $1.99 a minute, you can see her breasts, maybe her vagina, and you can stimulate yourself in a sad longing for deeper love.

"Step through another gate, and she will show you her outer gift-wrapping. She'll look at you with a certain twinkle in her eye. She'll answer your questions coyly. She'll give you just the faintest hint that there is more available.

"Step through another gate with your commitment, with your attention, with the small seedlings of devotion, and she'll open her heart to you more. She'll share with you her insecurities, the way that she's been hurt, her deepest longings. Some men will back away at this point. They realize that the price they must pay to go deeper is more than they are willing to give. They start to feel a responsibility. But for those few who step though another gate, they come to discover her loyalty, her willingness to stick with you no matter what, her willingness to raise your children, stick up for you in conversation, and, if you are lucky, even pick up your dirty socks now and then. And so it goes on. You've got the gist by now.

"Somewhere around the second wall from the center, she casts the veils of her personality aside, and shows you that she is both a human being and also a portal into something much greater than that. She shows you a wrath that is not hers, but all women's. She shows you a patience that is also universal. She shows you her wisdom. At this point you start to experience the archetypes of women, who have been portrayed as Goddesses and mythological figures in every tradition.

"Then, at the very center, in the innermost temple itself, all the layers of your devotion are flooded with reward all at once. You discover the very essence of the feminine, and in a strange way that is not exactly romantic, but profoundly sacred all the same, you realize that you could have gotten here with any woman if you had just been willing to pass through all the layers of initiation. Any woman is every woman, and every woman is any woman at the same time. When you love a woman completely, at the very essence of her being, this is the one Divine Feminine flame. It is what has made every woman in history beautiful. It's the flame behind the Mona Lisa, and Dante's Beatrice, and yes, also Penelope Cruz and Heidi Klum. You discover the magic ingredient which has led every man to fall in love with a woman.

"When you learn how to pay attention to the essence of the feminine in this way, you fall to the floor in full body prostration, tears soaking your cheeks and clothes, and you wonder how you could have ever taken Her, in all of Her forms, for granted even for a second."

We are fortunate to be living in a time when sexuality is coming back into the light after the dark ages of the '80s and '90s. Between AIDS and the Moral Majority, sex was to some extent a dangerous topic for both practice and discussion. Now that this period has run its course, we can embrace the present time and move forward with vigor. There are many resources and workshops for interested parties to avail themselves of as they begin their journey in Sacred Sexuality. It has become a movement that continues to gain momentum—and I am happy to be on the front line. I am embracing my leadership role with conviction. I stand for every woman and man who has lost the foundation of their life force which is sexual energy, and for every one of them who is returning to it. This is a legacy that we must pass on to future generations. It has never left the collective unconscious. It is an archetype. It is Truth.

Tantrica Maya is a creative force of nature. She has many talents and gifts with which she has made herself a comfortable life. She is also formally and self-educated in many fields including tantra. As an evolving life artist she chooses to leave herself defined as an open book. Her inspirations carry her along on her life journey. Her main website is www.TheEroticWay.com. You can join her on Facebook by following this link: www.facebook.com/#!/profile.php?id=1535212401

The Earth is the Goddess

By Susan Kornacki

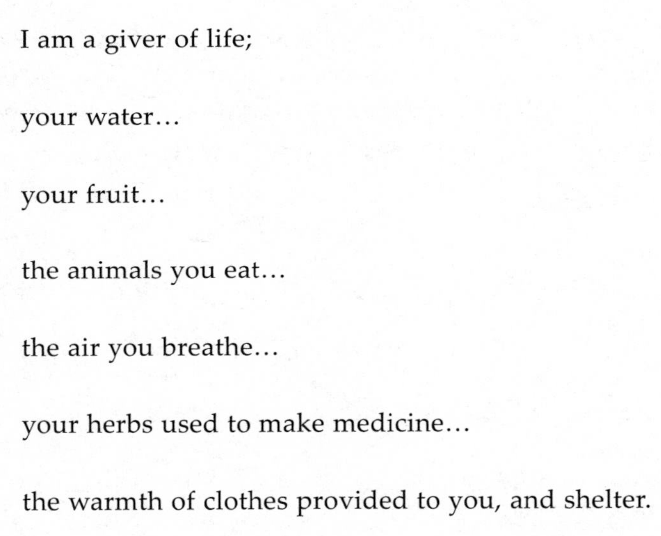

I am a giver of life;

your water…

your fruit…

the animals you eat…

the air you breathe…

your herbs used to make medicine…

the warmth of clothes provided to you, and shelter.

Who is tending to me? Who shows their gratitude? Who is using their consciousness to acknowledge I exist?

Who is protecting me?

We have a symbiotic relationship which allows us to grow and evolve together.

There is a perversion of this life energy in me now. I am sick and out of balance; too much damage, too many chemicals and structures used to control me instead of connecting in with me. Too much taken without anything given, and I am bleeding…So little attention given.

I was once a flourishing source of eternal love, bearer of fruit and giver of life because of the inter-relationship between us. Now I cannot sustain what has happened to me. There has been too much damage done. We have reached a critical point.

Man has treated me the same way that he treats the women on the planet and for this, now, we are all suffering.

Women are rising up out of the control and obligation bestowed upon them to "take care of man" in the current perverse imbalanced state that the male is in, and they are choosing to take care of their sisters and the Earth... to be warriors for themselves, each other, their children and the Mother Earth that they call home.

It is when man finds himself finally back in balance, that the woman can enter into a true relationship with the man. Only once she rises up and stakes her claim as a woman can she do this. She must say "no" to those impurities which have restricted the true divineness of the male and female energies flowing through her.

Where is man? Man is in ego and imbalanced. Generation after generation they are working for another man who works for another man, who works for another man, who works for another man... who is taking and forgetting to protect the bearer of fruit, the giver of life and the greatest nurturer of all. Man has forgotten his soul's job as a visitor on this planet: to protect the woman and the Earth.

I am Mother Earth. I am woman. I am the Divine Feminine and I am in need of other warriors to rise above the neglect, control and domination.

What would happen if we stopped working for man and worked for the Earth, our Mother? What would our connection with the cosmos and the primordial source energy look like then? What potential would we tap into for this, our evolution? Mother Earth is sick and it is time for a transformation.

"If you want to change the world....love a woman all the way through until she believes you, until her instincts, her visions, her voice, her art, her passion, her wildness have returned to her—until she is a force of love more powerful than all the political media demons who seek to devalue and destroy her."

Quote taken from the following source:)
http://www.magdalenewomen.com/love-a-woman

Susan A. Kornacki, from Boston, Massachusetts, is an emotional intelligence professional, lifetime experiencer of extraterrestrial energies, and deeply passionate about helping the Earth and mankind through this transition. By far the best job she's held is Mother and friend to her amazing eight year old daughter, Sidney J.

Lessons in Love

By Anonymous

It's been five years since an extremely painful series of relationships and breakups led to my having a multi-car accident that injured four people, myself included. Ironically, I had thought to myself just that morning that I was going to be able to make it, to go forward with my life (rather than go forward with my suicidal tendencies). I had come to believe that the theme of my life, namely love relationships—that which I had given the majority of my life force to for 40+ years—had been a series of mistakes and failures. I figured that life must not be about what I had thought it was. But what was it about then? Just working, just service? Just helping other people have a good life? Just watching others create something that I couldn't, no matter how hard I tried?

During these five years I stayed in a lot. The first year I had many chiropractic, massage, acupuncture and emotional healing sessions. I surrendered a lot of thoughts and dreams. I kept a lot of feelings to myself. I abandoned hope. I took up hope again. I abandoned it again. I told my minister friend that I was afraid to have another relationship, that it might end up in fatalities the next time, not just injuries. She said it wouldn't, to go ahead and try anyway.

Terrified of what might happen, I did online dating. I met a lot of weird people, and some nice people, online and off. The majority of them were also terrified, or at least really pissed off. No one died. But my dreams did become rather anemic. I wondered if my chances were over, if I would ever feel that kind of connection again. And if I did, was it just old addictive behavior, more fooling myself? In the meantime, my newly widowed minister friend did online dating herself, fell in love and got married. She said she had done nothing extraordinary, but to me it seemed truly amazing.

One of the men I'd met online was sweet, smart, friendly, creative… and bipolar. He was on Social Security disability for it. I can see the beauty in all kinds of people, but I'd had a bipolar boyfriend before and it had been disastrous. So I knew not to go there again. There was just one problem: he was the only man I had felt attracted to in years. I dated him as a friend for a while. Then he didn't call for a month. I thought that was for the best.

Then he came around again. After having a dream that I felt was telling me I would only hurt him if we kept seeing each other, I told him it was over. He handled it beautifully and said he understood. Two months later he called, on both my phones. I didn't answer. Then he emailed me. I wrote back and said he could come over sometime and hold me. He showed up and was so happy that we were together again, that I didn't tell him we weren't. Something had shifted, and he had my attention in a new way.

During our time apart, he had dated other women and done significant releasing of old attachments. What had shifted for me was the realization that it was actually me, not him, that I was afraid of hurting.

The other thing that had transpired was that a girlfriend helped me to do a "love spell". It included candles, affirmations, ribbons, flowers and fragrant oils. It was a ritual she and I planned out and did together. I think the most powerful part was the "homework". She had me write down a list of the things my future Beloved would say to me. I can tell you they were very different from the things my ex-husband had been saying! For example: "You are the most beautiful woman in the world to me, and the only one I want to be with for the rest of my life!"

When my new friend then started saying those very things to me, I was amazed. And it was a good thing I had written them down. I realized that if I'd heard a guy saying those things to me in the past, I would have thought he was kind of "dumb". I guess I hadn't thought that loving me was actually a smart thing to do. No wonder I wasn't finding my partner!

But bipolar? Yes, he has been, but he is also now controlled, and vigilant about his processes, states and medications. He is creative and successful in many ways, and consistently positive and open. He has been stable now for a few years. He has repaired his damaged relationships with his three grown children, and I figure that probably says as much as anything could. He is interested in his continued healing, of body, mind and spirit. He is willing to do whatever he can to facilitate my healing.

I am aware that things may change, so I am conscious of staying in the present and just appreciating being loved in the ways that I want to be loved. And how is he loving me? What is keeping me with a man who is such an uncertain endeavor? Well, I know that in his eyes I am beautiful, in all ways, and he reminds me regularly. He wakes from a sound sleep, looks my way and says, "You're so pretty!" It's a nice way to start the day. And I know that he means it.

For a year now he has been consistent. He respects my space. I have a private bedroom that I have not invited him into. Yet. Other men had found reasons to peek in or trick their way in. He says he doesn't want to see or go in unless I want him to. He listens to me. He LISTENS. What I say is important to him. All kinds of things. Even when I can't stand what I am saying, when I am being compulsive, micro-managing and insecure, he tells me I'm ok. He is relaxed and admiring. He has an openness to and appreciation of my ideas and endeavors, whether they involve him or not.

And once, when I was at a church dinner that had a dessert bar and I had a plate full of desserts, a girlfriend told me I'd be as big as a house if I ate all that. He leaned over and whispered,

"Eat all you want." I thought then that I might be in love! :-). Then, when I made a healthy choice to go off sugar for a while, he decided to do it too. And that's been over a month now, including Christmas!

This guy is definitely not perfect. He has sleep apnea, which made him snore like a train, at least before he quit sugar. It's so much better now, though not gone entirely. He has a low paying job, but he is a willing worker. He has my same issues of codependence, overly caring for others to the neglect of self, and we monitor that behavior in the mirror of each other. He has times of confusion and uncertainty. But he talks about them, owns them and works through them. I am convinced that he is truly loving his life and me the best he can, and is working to learn how to do it better.

After half a lifetime of romantic fantasies and endeavors, which included several engagements, marriages, children, moving across the country, writing songs, poetry, working together, traveling, open relationships, group relationships, same-sex relationships, age differences, racial differences, lack of self respect, tolerating abuse, being dramatic and abusive myself, and numerous breakups—all finally leading to my car accident and injuries—I came to make some changes. Maybe I'm a slow learner. I finally took time off from relationships. I didn't want to, but that's how addicts are. And yes, I joined Sex, Love, and Relationship Addicts Anonymous, which involved phone meetings and Serenity Prayers. I was determined that, in order to live, and for the people around me to be safe too, I would change my ways.

So now I am trying this. And I like it. So far, so good. I'm not rushing into anything (I hope). I'm going through the seasons and allowing the situation to unfold. I'm balancing on my own two feet, so that I will still be standing if this relationship ends. I am grateful for each day of being loved by this sweetest of men. More than ever before, I am committed to the Divine in myself, and to whatever situation most honors Her. Will it be this relationship? We'll see.

Exploring Tantra

An interview with Maya Yonika, subject of the movie "Sex Magic—Manifesting Maya". (Questions asked by Gabriel Morris via email.)

Talk about how you first got involved with tantra.

I think I came from the womb with the innate mission of questioning the validity of just about everything. But where the angels and demons most whispered secrets into my ears was in the realms of sex and relationships. When I became involved with Tantra, I was in need, at the deepest soul level, of experiencing depth and meaning in those places. I was looking everywhere I knew, trying to find healthier ways of being. And although Tantra wasn't one of the directions I was searching, the lessons we need have a way of finding us. I'll share with you two core circumstances that ultimately brought Tantra to me.

There was a period, perhaps a year or so after acquiring my Bachelor's degree, that I was riding my bike to work every morning to a little coffee shop in Austin, Texas. Every day on that ride, I passed a 'Gentleman's Club'… and every day, as I passed by, my stomach would tighten. I was bothered by the reality that, throughout university, I had paid my own way, working really hard to achieve that certificate in good standing… yet there I was, still working at a coffee shop for minimum wage, still struggling to make rent. Since leaving home at 15, I'd had a hell of a time trying to survive in the world, so I was feeling a bit anxious as it was sinking in that the Bachelor's—my vestige of hope towards ascension from minimalism and poverty—was proving to amount to nothing except... debt! How unjust is that?! Meanwhile, I knew that inside that club, there were girls… *those* kinds of girls… making more in one night then I did in an entire week. So there I was, a complete ass, supposedly doing the 'right' thing; and yet I was broke, angry and mega bored with the whole thing.

Beyond all that…what was up with these men? Even from childhood I wondered where values and ethics came into play; with people, with the environment, money, work. Yet it was the strip clubs, porn and the sex trade industries that were rolling in the dough. Why were the men here, rather than caring for their children, homes or communities? Was it just me? Had I watched too many episodes of 'Little House on the Prairie' and 'Grizzly Adams'? Whatever it was, I was at the end of my rope with 'survival mode', especially considering I'd done 'the right things', and I was still in it.

But just as daunting was the level of judgment I had toward everything about that stupid place. Whether it was truly as evil as I thought or not, at the same time that I was judging it, I also didn't like the fact that I had a sense of hatred towards it going on. And although I didn't understand it at the time, the intensity of my repulsion somehow turned it around and made it more about me.

So one day I parked my bike outside, went in and filled out an application. I was painfully aware that I couldn't stand another day in the powerlessness that was strangling my life like some ethereal python from hell. So I cut hours at the coffee house, maintaining just enough work to pose some semblance of social accountability; and went out shopping for G-strings and 6-inch heels. How, I pondered aghast, dangling before me a pair of sparkling red 'fuck me' pumps, was I to walk in these things, let alone dance? I was an alchemical soup of excitement, curiosity and sheer terror for the stage I was about to step onto. Do I get to practice a little first? What do I do with the pole?… Yet, despite my complete lack of experience in the matter, I got the job.

Meanwhile, the angels and demons had been busy

whispering their antics to me at home as well. I was traversing through new themes from the same vein. There, for the first time, my partner and I were experimenting in the world of polyamory. I'll tell you why…

Perhaps typical relationship standards in the west are considered 'normal' to most folk. But to me, it was all looking rather devastating. I just didn't get it. I was always either scared or bored or angry or obsessing. I didn't have one iota of calm or contentedness or centeredness… or the slightest idea what it meant to just stop, and enjoy creation… grounded in my own well-being and direction. I was something akin to an abused Chihuahua on methamphetamines.

I didn't know if it was my own childhood experience or else the undercurrents of control, manipulation, jealousy, anger, resentment, and general unpleasantness that I was noticing all around me. But it all left me wondering what any of it had to do with love. I mean, how did hardly anything society was spitting out relate to love? I remember as a kid in elementary school, staring blankly into a list of possible careers. The other kids were happily checking their boxes: fireman, policeman, architect, secretary. I just couldn't fit myself into any of them. I looked around wondering what was wrong with me… and continued feeling like that for many years to come.

The only conceivable paths I knew of to a better way were: A) The Conventional Model—Psychotherapy, or B) The Alternative—Polyamory. I'd tried psychotherapy enough already to know how useful it was… so what remained was the alternative. Polyamory wasn't something I was excited about. I wasn't sure it was even ethical. But what I was sure of at that time, was that I was in partnership with a man who, although I loved him dearly, was burning a flame of a lesser caliber, and my bored gene was kicking in. We both knew something had to change, but we weren't so interested in separating.

Funny enough, a few years back I'd happened to meet a

polyamorous man who was well spoken, charismatic, well educated, well traveled, completely intriguing, and delightfully sexy… and who happened to be completely crazy about me. He also had a beautiful wife of similarly endearing qualities. It was the perfect opportunity to give poly a try. So, I presented the idea to my partner, and he agreed… albeit hesitantly.

I've got these two situations in my life going on backstage, as it were. Life is looking a little different. Several months pass, and some nights in the club are close to enjoyable in between the shady layers. Sometimes I like dancing on stage, and on a good night I find meaning in giving attention to some of the men. Compassionate understanding… in between 'sleaze ball' accusations made under my breath… slowly replaces my judgment for strip clubs. And I'm putting decent money in my pocket for the first time ever. So on some days I get to go to the coffee shop just to lounge around, read books, and drink latte.

However there's a slight problem. I'm an ex alcoholic and drug addict, and the strip club is swarming with my demons. But really, who can work a night at a strip club without a drink or two? I contain myself well enough and never get drunk. Nevertheless, the place is always filled with cigarette smoke, and even two drinks a night is beyond what my body appreciates, so I'm getting sick… slowly and steadily. Meanwhile, in my explorations of polyamory I'm walking on the edge between blunders and blissful encounters. We always love the other couple's company. And there's something completely wonderful about the unstated agreement that we all make love to each other, even when we're loving another. However, that's an ideal that doesn't always work out as planned or expected. I hardly notice that my partner is growing even more distant from me… until it's too late. So after some time, as the newness wears off and I look around, I come to figure out that, even though there's been some really sweet sexual sharing, the thing that I was missing all along… something, I don't know, emotional I guess… is still missing. Plus I'm just feeling like crap. The self-judgment starts coming in big, because... well... what now? The stripping is great money, but it makes me sick. The poly is fun and sexual, but still something's not right. So what else to do at that point, but fall into a deep pit of depression?

In the midst of all this, I've been speaking with a friend I knew from the festival circuit a few years back, named Desert, or "Dez" for short. Dez calls himself a 'Tantric Sacred Sexual Healer', and he's been talking me through my challenges in open relationship and in the strip club the entire time, which has been nothing less than a Godsend. I call him any time I feel I can't take another step forward... which is quite regularly at this point. His words help me to keep my chin up for another day. Meanwhile, he's also been telling me that he thinks I'm "oh so very special". So special, in fact, that he thinks I'm what you call a *Dakini* (tantric adept) and, you never know, maybe he and I are meant to be partners? And what if I came to his temple in Sedona to be with him? And hey, what if we were to travel and teach Tantra together! Wouldn't that be cool?

My thoughts on this are that I think he's been very helpful to me... but I know absolutely nothing about Tantra. But shit, come to think of it, I wish that I did because all of that sounds really amazing and profound. Is he serious? He can't be. But even if he is, one little problem with the whole idea is that I'm pretty sure he's a major player. And I'm not into that.

But then something else happens. Just when things are pretty bad, they get much worse. My brother passes away from a massive head aneurism.

I spend the next six months becoming part of the living room furniture. I still work as a stripper, as minimally as possible. And I still see my other lover, but doing my best to push him away. My primary relationship has since fallen apart and I'm now sleeping in the office. Both of them are available sexually if I'd like, but the notion of being sexual just for sex's sake makes my stomach turn.

I need something… rich, connected, deep… something I don't have, or know how to express, or ask for... even to myself. I don't think anything I'm doing is right. I'm still depressed, and exhausted, and I don't know what to do.

It's like if there's a drill sergeant in your face screaming "DO IT SOLDIER!"...but not telling you what to do, so all you can do is stand there and take it. The drill sergeant doesn't give a shit that you're exhausted and beat and life has no meaning.

There were two people in this world that I felt I could say anything to. And now one of them is gone. The other one has left me an invite in my email inbox: "Come with me to travel the world and teach Tantra." Well…what did I have to lose?

Sum up the events and experiences in the movie, just to give the readers a general idea of what it's about.

Daka falls in love with girl. Daka tells girl she's a Dakini. He is a practitioner of 'Tantra' and calls sex and relationships 'Sacred'. And she has for a long time been holding a deep calling inside of her to understand and embody that truth. He lavishes her with attention, calls her 'Goddess', and she thinks he offers the kind of life experience and meaningful work that makes her eyes brighten and her toes wiggle. So they come together in a poly relationship and travel the world and teach Tantra: meaning, Daka teaches workshops, Dakini listens and adds in her two cents, and people really dig on it.

Dakini starts feeling uneasy because Daka is having sex with overwhelming numbers of women. But the thing is, he has many years of experience in this work and is changing lives around the world. He battles the constrictive binds of sexual conditioning, and is a healer of sexual wounding. He speaks of the temples of old and the distorted masculine and wounded feminine, and the need to end separation. He offers sacred spot massage and 'Sacred Union'. Orgasms mean healing… the more the better. He has a 'big sexual appetite' and desires 'beautiful Goddesses'—

lots of them. He is a lover and a fighter for sexual freedom!

There are issues for others around this, but he has no issues. In fact, he's walking into this 'fully aware'… 'taking total responsibility'. After all, somebody's got to do this! It is women's issues of jealousy and separation that must be healed when contracted in the face of his sexual appetite. How can I really argue with that. I mean, lots of women were enjoying their time with him. Aren't I just being a selfish ninny to want him to slow down and be there with me?

For about a year and a half I shared a relationship with him in which one lover followed the next in a never-ending train. I was rather shell-shocked over the first few months, as I realized the extent of what I was becoming involved in, since I hadn't realized that this level of poly actually existed. But there I was in the middle of it, and our life was in such constant motion that the best I could do was go along with it, and learn to confront 'my issues', as he so generously pointed out.

Granted, I wasn't always great at that, seeing as this was quite a confusing situation. Were these truly only *my* issues? Or were some of them *his* perhaps? Projections? Or just plain bullshit? But he's a 'big person' who knows lots of other big people with lots of big stuff going on. And this is the biggest I've ever been… with more money, travel, experience and recognition than I've ever experienced. And I'd come to really love Dez.

But, what the hell was wrong with him? Wasn't he clearly a sex addict? And if not, why couldn't he just chill the fuck out and be with me? I was sure that he was, but who was I to say? Something was wrong here, and after a while it became more and more apparent that it wasn't just me.

Towards the end of our time together, my humor was dead gone. I felt sucked dry and had lost any last vestiges of hope or interest in him. It's not that I wasn't willing, but man, there just wasn't any real space from one of his lovers to the next for me to actually chill out and feel nurtured in our partnership.

By the time I'd decided I was at the end of my rope, it was already too late. I was hanging from a thread that was quickly shredding with disgust. When I found I could no longer stand the smell of him or even his room… that's when I finally left the relationship.

But I was shocked at how upset he got when I left. He's crying… seemingly traumatized. This baffles me. What would he be missing, amidst his dozens of other lovers? After all, to him… well… I haven't been able to get beyond my issues to truly meet him. I've heard that so many times and looked at it so much that I've grown numb to it now. He says he's never loved a woman like this before. He can't get over me. But I'm beyond over it. I'm cooked, toast.

After I'm out of the picture, the film still needs to roll. Dez starts using Sex Magic with other lovers and clients to call me back into his life. Although I'm gone, I remain in confusion around the disparity between his words and actions. He seems to somehow exist in my 'field' all the time. I wonder why he's still there. I know that I'm not wanting to be with him. But his conviction about our partnership when I speak with him still makes me wonder… has it really all just been my issues? But deep down I know what I have seen and experienced.

Nevertheless my confusion and lack of clarity brings me back for a visit to see how we feel. When I arrive, we lay together and we feel good there, and it seems to be a bit of a breakthrough. I can actually relax around him this time, and I consider the possibility of allowing him back into my life. After all, a few weeks ago he'd gone out and bought an engagement ring and asked for my hand in marriage, saying things would be different. I thought about that for a moment as I gazed at that ring, and told him I'd sit with it a few days.

It's at this juncture, shown in the movie, when Dez's client and lover, Robin, is shown all teary eyed and grateful at how beautiful it is that she had helped with Sex Magic to bring me back into Dez's life. Yeah, thanks, Robin... you meant well...

But no, I don't go back. I know better now. Beyond his words and a momentary experience of goodness between us, I've developed a good strong distrust for him. So I walk away for good this time.

What were the qualities of Baba Dez that led you to become involved with him in the beginning? Was it mostly a matter of him being a good lover and a teacher of tantra, or did it go well beyond sex and the physical?

I was in a very challenged place when we came into partnership. And although I'd proceeded with bells and whistles and red flags of warning, those could be overlooked and justified, seeing that there was so much being offered. First and foremost was the beautiful image of a life practice that brought spirituality and sexuality together. Up until that point, I'd never really amounted to much, but a serious pain in the ass, to whichever poor soul took me on as their girlfriend.

But how amazing was all this. Now I was going to learn to be a real, live Dakini! So what led me was that deep need... into the rich, rooted, earthy nurturance of meaning. I was willing to tolerate his sexual proclivities at first (though I had no idea the true extent of it) considering it was all in the realms of what I was exploring. I wanted to know healthy, conscious relationship. His esoteric jargon: 'tantra', 'sacred sex', 'divine feminine'... all of that had me thinking that here were the keys. And it was all wrapped up neatly in a silk cloth, tied with a bow and presented on a silver platter.

As for sexuality, physically we were a perfect fit. Many people commented on how beautifully we matched each other. Energetically, however, was a different story. And there would be major lessons around this... lessons that I am still learning from, years later. Nevertheless, the first night we made love and slept together in his bed, I had an amazingly vivid dream. It was of an intensely bright double rainbow—something I'd never actually seen in waking life, until later that year in our travels to Australia together. It was so clear that regardless of any doubts or red flags I may have had… this was an undoubtedly clear omen. I felt I was exactly where I was supposed to be.

What's your understanding of the real meaning of Tantra? And how does or doesn't Tantra relate to "sacred sexuality"?

First of all, if we're going to delve into the real meaning of Tantra, I shall begin with the following disclaimer: I know absolutely nothing of and do not claim authority or expertise on 'real' Tantric knowledge. I don't follow any specific sect; nor have I, in this lifetime, been a devotee of any Tantric teacher… well, except a boyfriend or two. But maybe that was just obsession. Believe you me, if I'd had the chance, I would have jumped at the opportunity, considering how I was motivated by a longing to surrender into the comfort and safety of such guidance.

However it doesn't always work out the way we think we want it… and thank God for that. That said, if you are to place yourself voluntarily on a Tantric path without a guru, you'll need a peculiar combination of masochistic fearlessness of the warrior, innate humility and a wise devotional intent that guides your path. You must have the will to go where angels fear to tread—and that place is usually not of your own bidding. It is sitting in the metaphorical cremation grounds, that transforms fear and confusion into the greatest of Gifts… which is the very impetus to recognize 'I Am'. It's one hell of a ride. I won't pretty it up for you. It can take years or a day or a lifetime to walk through. But once you do, Magic becomes normal, and one comes to peace with all of the challenges faced as rites and gifts set out by the One True guru. Disclaimer made…

I like the description of Tantra as 'madhuvidya'—the 'honey teachings'. This means that the bees of Spirit do the work of transforming all that is—good and evil, dark and light, the beautiful and the ugly—into nectar. Tantric knowledge and initiations are traditionally handed down from a guru to a disciple, and incorporate long periods of discipline and practice, utilizing strict ethical codes, yoga, meditation, mantra, yantra and rituals. Disciplines bring the mind and body into harmony with Spirit, unlocking creative potentials, cultivating evolutionary thought, and providing the strength and will power to journey alone into the depths of the unknown to find our own unique truths and wisdom.

The Left Hand Path, or Red Tantra, utilizes sexual ritual for the purpose of achieving liberation from desire and attachment, while the Right Hand Path, or White Tantra, is generally an ascetic and celibate path with the same aim. Tantra utilizes the body and the mundane world as access to the Spiritual. A path of non-duality, the self is seen as a microcosm of all that is. Physical reality and the mundane become Sacred… and all aspects of creation are seen as Divine. This is what I understand as 'real' Tantra.

Tantra in the West, however, is furtively called Neo-Tantra, pop or California Tantra. It is a beautiful effort to bring intimacy and human connection back into a collective on a perfectly devastating prosaic trajectory. It is a profound body of work that effectively addresses the sparks of Spiritual awakening…manifest as both urgent desires for corporeal comfort of sexuality, and the need to submerge oneself into the unknown. Yet Neo-Tantra has earned its name well, as its teachings tend to enfold upon itself; oftentimes caught within the 'lower triangle' consciousness in practice, as is the apprehension of so many of its teachers. They are, after all, receiving money, sex and power. It remains stuck because it is a neophyte—sprouted directly from the soil of a materially bound, spiritually pretentious and sexually obsessive paradigm.

Because Neo-Tantra lacks the most pertinent aspects of Tantra, it doesn't know what it doesn't know, and if it were to open its eyes it would find itself stuck in the same patterns of ego and gratification, sitting on the opposite polarity of the very culture it seeks to heal...which is the same place that it started. More abundance, more love, more sex, more orgasms... does this all sound familiar?

Professing non-duality, it nevertheless egotistically sees itself as the healer of a sexually sick culture. And so in its wake, it can perpetuate the very sickness it projects outwards to attempt to heal. It is Tantra's scantily-dressed, pothead teenager... bouncing excitedly around its father's perimeters, borrowing his language and imparting his movements in pretense of maturity. It thinks it can seduce and fuck itself into the depths it yearns for, but doesn't yet understand.

Nevertheless, what Neo-tantra is addressing cannot be avoided. How we experience and understand sexuality determines the experiences of our lives. If we are to evolve Spiritually, we must look at where we are deeply conditioned sexually, face our shadows and reprogram ourselves into a more authentic sexuality. But we cannot do that if we are simply following yet another collective conditioning. One must eventually step out of the safety of egoistic identities, and move beyond the spiritually idealistic, sweet sounding, yet surface level Spiritual clichés. Eventually everyone must come to sit in the cremation grounds, alone... and face Death. But what a party pooper I am! Isn't the pleasure paradigm delicious? Life is everything. Everything is Tantra...even Neo-Tantra. Did I just contradict myself?

It would behoove Neo-Tantra's practitioners to stand tall and proud without guiltily hiding behind the word 'Tantra'—a discipline who's breadth it does not fully honor—and remain within a more honest portrayal of what it is: 'Sacred Sexuality'. That said, those tantric honeybees do have a way of transforming 'All that is' in just the right ways. Everything exactly as it is, is absolutely perfect.

Talk a little about sex and boundaries. At what point did you realize the relationship with Baba Dez wasn't what you wanted, and even that it had crossed into the realm of being unbalanced and unhealthy? From your perspective now, is polyamory not the right way to go, either in general or for you personally? Does it go against the nature of human needs for emotional commitment and stability, or do you still think it can be a balanced and workable lifestyle under the right circumstances?

First and foremost, one must truly know oneself— expectations, desires, intentions and goals—to have clear boundaries. If we haven't yet delved into our deepest internal/shadow work, then what we call 'boundaries' are more appropriately termed 'walls'. They are the inflexible, reactive places manifested from the pain and fear created from childhood wounds and cultural conditioning, arising from the subconscious. Along the path of our journey, ideally we learn to break down the solidity of these walls, and create clear, flexible boundaries...usually by crossing over them.

From the beginning I didn't think partnership with Dez was ultimately what I wanted. But I also wasn't completely sure. He was fun and a helpful friend. But I wasn't so deeply attracted, and I'd had red flags about his sexual nature from the start. But the thing is, the essence behind those flags was alluring; meaning, I wanted to understand how to be less emotional and attached. At the same time, I wanted to find a sense of depth and meaning in work, and in life. I wanted to be Spiritual... But I'm the prozac poster child.

The way I figured it, if anyone could show me the ropes, it was a man with the title 'Tantric Sacred Sexual Healer'. And at the same time, that man was clear that I was a Dakini. So the dynamic we have here... is a girl without a daddy, and a man with some kind of 'authority' telling this girl she's special in some way. You get the picture.

Anyway, seeing I wasn't that into him, this would be the perfect opportunity to explore all of this. Of course, within the first week together we became glued at the hip every second. But he has other lovers and plans ahead, and before much longer, that confidently detached coolness is slipping between my fingers. Suddenly I find myself entangled in a complex and baffling web of thoughts, emotions, feelings, intuitions and sexual energetic strings and snares that I just hadn't planned on at all… or had I?

Nevertheless, as we travel the world together, holding workshops and discussions, I'm sitting tall next to him, in the important Spiritual person seat, and loving everything I'm hearing. This was all completely new language, and all very exciting!

Yet, as time rolled along, the man introducing concepts like 'the body, heart and belly knows', was the very person that my belly was slowly contracting in response to. While he's saying 'sex is Sacred', I'm not so certain that he's treating it that way. A major inward struggle with myself ensues between the opposing messages of body and mind, Spiritual and emotional, logical and intuitive.

Nevertheless, I wanted to be healthy and conscious more than anything. My highest priority was to face my shadows and projections. So each time I felt triggered around his sexuality with other women, I did my best to look at my wounds, jealousy and anger. I punched pillows and slammed my face into them screaming "You asshole!" I processed with others. I cried and ached and moaned. I climbed mountains, studied metaphysics, did cleansing and colonics, and ate lots and lots of spirulina.

Over time, with the constant train of women that kept coming and coming, I guess I was holding out hope that he would one day just 'snap out of it'. I couldn't understand his choice of perpetual distraction with other women vs. giving it a rest and going deeper with the one who he repeatedly claimed to love the most… who was clearly distraught and asking him to stop and be with her.

So as I mulled over the tits and ass 'Tantric massage' ads, the question kept returning: "how is any of this Sacred?" But there was so much tempting me to stay: the words, the vision, the travel, the money in my pocket and some sorely needed attention and recognition. All that kept me doing my best to recognize what I was being told through his 'authority' and 'expertise' on these subjects, that it was my own issues that kept me questioning and contracted… my pain, judgment and fear around sexuality.

So when did I know the relationship with Baba Dez wasn't what I wanted? That would depend on which part of me you asked. But I think that in my heart, I knew from the start. Yet our deepest Soul's lessons are not always so gentle. In the end, it was those red flags that ultimately became the finger pointing to the moon… to face the frightening, challenging and unknown places, bring down the walls and experience the humanity that exists in those places. One day, years down the line, I could integrate and transform it all into a wiser, more compassionate and loving place.

I could easily enough say, from one perspective, that the entire relationship was 'unhealthy' and 'unbalanced'. But what would be the point in that? I'd rather say that those experiences led me through the Valley of the Shadow of Death. Those lessons forced me to open my eyes and bring myself into my freedom and power. My life has improved tremendously since, so ultimately, it was the most healthy and rewarding relationship I've experienced.

In terms of polyamory, I think for some, poly is certainly the way to go. After all, how could it not be? There are many doing it! I know a handful of couples who have been successfully poly for years. I think what creates that success is a very strong foundational partnership. They raise children together, are dynamic in their individual careers, and carry a certain level of maturity in supporting each other equally. With such solid foundations, no... I don't feel it necessarily goes against needs for emotional commitment and stability. If that is the path that interests them, and they mutually meet one another in that desire, then that is theirs to experience.

Yet for me, it's not what I ultimately want—mainly because what I have encountered so much in the poly community is a tendency towards an intense focus on sexuality and relationships. For me, that focus has become rather annoying and redundant. Beyond this, in my own experience in poly relationship, I never quite encountered that "God I just can't contain myself, I am so in love I can barely stay inside my skin, eyes welling, my heart is exploding, dripping with love" kind of experience. And for me, being immersed in someone that way, in the juicy depths of such intense passion, is what really makes life worth living. And I'd rather wait to have that, even if just for one more experience in this lifetime, than have all the sex in the world that never quite rises to that level. I've only had that experience of meeting another in that way with monogamous partners, as we've grown deeper in love with each other over time. But that's just been my experience. Who is to say what is yet to come?

From a practical perspective, polyamory makes absolute sense under plenty of circumstances. For example, imagine if couples with children, finding themselves at odds, considered the choice to remain together working as a parental team, while opening their relationships to others in order to find greater satisfaction, thus avoiding having to break up the partnership? Can you imagine how much healthier those children's perspectives would be... how much more safe, nurtured and loved they will feel?

What if partners love each other and wish to remain together, yet clearly are changing, perhaps sexually or spiritually, in incompatible directions and desire to be met by another in those changes? With some alternative reference points and a little creative thought towards options other than jumping to divorce or vindictive separations, the world becomes a place of limitless possibilities. Judging any path as right or wrong for everyone is just stupid. Now, many a polyamorist is just as guilty as the monogamists for their righteous indignation and finger wagging. My question for polyamory from a spiritual perspective is—is poly and sex being used to avoid and distract from higher consciousness, or else to move closer? This is up to each individual to decide.

For me, poly was a finger pointing to the moon… ultimately directing me towards the depths of connection with myself and All That Is that I was seeking from the very beginning. I just didn't know it. Sex and Spirit are inseparable, and it is way too easy to call one or the other blasphemous according to their own narrowed terms. Sex can be one of the most beautiful, pleasurable and profound paths to God. Yet, as with any medicine, ceremony, religion or even philosophy, more does not always equal better. Deep honoring and discretion must be taken for the power of such a potent gift—lest it turn to poison.

Do you still practice tantra in some form, and if so what does it entail?

You know, I used to try, very hard, to understand Tantra and to work at being a Tantric. I went to the workshops and conferences, traveled around the world thinking I was going to heal myself and help heal other people. But now I think that the practice of Tantra only really begins when we drop all of that, realizing there's nothing to heal. The time came that I forgot I was seeking… and the understanding of God within All That Is somehow evolved from a mental concept, into an embodied reality. That is the Tantra that I now experience.

What is sex magic and how does it fit into tantra, if at all?
Sex magic is the use of orgasmic energy for prayer. It is extremely powerful. And yes, it can be used Tantrically. However, that would entail its use only by the wisest and most developed beings who have 'squashed the grapes of ego so they may partake in the wine of Spirit'.

Wielded for the purpose of satisfying ego's desires... it is otherwise known as Black Magic. The present fad of teaching Sex Magic to any workshop attendee is like handing a two-year-old a canister of gasoline and a pack of matches. It is justified with a surface level of spiritual idealism, and utterly ignorant towards the energies inherent in such a practice. I have heard too many teachers justify the use of Sexual or Black Magic by using such words as 'if it be for the highest good'. Yet, can you imagine the otherworldly, elemental forces would discern and pick out such a phrase that was uttered... rather than the profoundly passionate depth of one's innermost feelings, thoughts, desires, distortions and Soul energies being broadcast by that person in the throes of sexual union? It's akin to saying that you can look a person in the eye and say 'fuck you', and it doesn't matter what energy is coming through. When in truth, that 'fuck you' could be anywhere on the spectrum from hilarious to vicious or beyond. The words themselves are not the truth. The truth emanates as an energy from within.

After everything you've experienced, what are your thoughts on sex as it fits into the scheme of life? Are we all just overly obsessed with it and making it out to be more than it really is, or does it still live up to all the hype for you? And did you ever reach something you might call ultimate sexual satisfaction? If so, how or why—was it more of a physical experience, an emotional one, a spiritual revelation, all of the above or something entirely indescribable perhaps?
I feel that, yes—we as a society are undoubtedly obsessed with

sex. Yet, sexuality and relational forms are, historically, the fulcrum point of cultural structure. With the massive shifts in paradigm that are now occurring, I think this focus on sexuality is serving the purpose of waking us up from prosaic structures of nuclear family, individualism, isolation, separation and the meaninglessness that has been created through all of this. Perhaps this 'obsessive' focus is the interpretation of Shakti stirring a culture that's running on the lower three chakras.

As I said a bit earlier, for me, all the hype on sexuality has grown redundant. I feel the same for all the hype about spirituality, as well. There's a whole lot of lip service pointing to something that is still missing… whether it be 'Sacred Sex', 'Tantra', 'Spiritual integration' or what have you. We've become dumb with spiritually prosaic phrases. A good friend, in fact, recently wrote me, frustrated about this very subject: "I get the feeling that these well-worn 'loving' clichéd phrases are just a substitute for feeling the pain of not yet being where these people want to be—with 'God', enlightened, happy, etc." My point is simply that there exists a radical difference between integrated embodiment, and hype. So no, the hype is not so interesting.

As for the 'ultimate sexual experience' I will say this: I've had many profound sexual experiences in the past. Those experiences were simply my natural expression at the time. Since then, I've become a different being, seeing the roles of love and sexuality in an entirely new way. Yet I've been on my own for most of my deepest integrations over the last few years, and now I'm just being here, doing as I love. So, whether my sexual experiences in the future will become something other than what I have experienced so far, is yet to be seen. The 'ultimate sexual satisfaction' at present is simply acceptance of what is...nothing else needed.

What advice can you convey to men in the general realm of relating with women? What can or should men do better or differently in order to connect with women in the same way

that women desire in their hearts to connect with men?

Any man will be able to connect with a woman when he is truly connected with himself. Problem is, most people are so caught up in their stories that they can't get quiet enough to center, step outside of their dramas, and offer to themselves what they need in order to create the changes that will truly alter their lives. Men who are connected to Nature, Earth, and devotion have no problems relating here. He must be willing to walk through the Valley of the Shadow of Death in order to come into his maturity. And that may very well mean walking alone and learning that the energy and pleasure of Shakti is from Source… all that is… not from the physical womb—just as all women must learn that the stability and protection of Consciousness is from Spirit, not from a man. When a man does this… when he is connected with the nature of his True devoted Self, he will not need to 'do anything' differently. He will simply be different within…and naturally know how to connect with and deeply love woman.

What advice or tips can you give men when it comes to lovemaking? What do men generally do wrong, what do they do right, and what should they be doing that they just aren't getting around to at all? What are a few super important things that men should keep in mind when it comes to making love, that will help take both man and woman into something resembling cosmic ecstasy, true sexual satisfaction?

So I'm gonna answer this question for both men and women. Feeling the depths of love cannot be omitted from lovemaking, if it is to be truly ecstatic and satisfying. It is vulnerability, openness and the willingness to experience and dance with whatever arises naturally that is needed. Our sexuality is so metaphorical for where we are as a collective. What we generally do 'wrong' is focus on the physical. We go into constant motion because our nervous systems are wound up and we are so conditioned to going for the goal… when the best part is along the journey. We don't need to try… it is always felt.

Trying to make a woman come or stay hard or get to orgasm is the antithesis of the most profound levels of sensuality. When we try and move into constant physical, goal oriented sex, our genitals, our hearts and our souls grow numb. 'Trying' needs to be replaced with being, and being can only transpire when we are integrated enough in ourselves to truly relax into love. Then the focus is on the entire experience, not just the genitals, or the erection, or the orgasm. Then we begin to slow down, feeling ourselves and our partners… honoring the love that is there, the mystery of being in these bodies, eye to eye, deeply present… moving with the natural waves and rhythms of what is.

What is the true nature or role of femininity as you see it, the goddess energy, and what is or should be the real role of the masculine?

This is a tricky question to respond to, as masculine and feminine are forever One, inseparable Beingness. Nevertheless, I will do my best to outline a distinction. Know that any 'roles' portrayed are absolute bullshit and mental concepts that, if taken literally, ultimately serve as nothing but entrapment.

That said, the feminine is limitless, feeling, flowing, creativity in action and manifestation. She cannot be separated from the masculine, as she embodies him. She is consciousness itself, manifest. If I look at mother nature, Gaia… I can see her fecundity, her loving and giving nature. She is a limitless source of beauty and creativity that nurtures and provides. She provides joyously for those who honor her natural beauty, flow and rhythms, providing everything we need. Yet if she is seen as separate, if her gifts are forgotten and dishonored as something to greedily take from, she responds with great force, either becoming dry, deserted and barren… or a raging storm that destroys everything in its wake.

So her role embodies both sexuality and death—to nurture,

provide and birth creation into being, as well as provide the energy and form needed to catalyze the lessons of Spiritual growth and learning. The masculine is Spirit, Truth… unchanging consciousness itself. He cannot be separated from the Goddess Shakti, as he is the Ultimate Source of her form. He is life and breath itself. The masculine is the Father, who provides truth, wisdom, structure, direction, knowing… the seed of life. Every cell, tree, plant, fish and animal knows what to do. They simply are what they are… they be… as consciousness itself.

Only man developed the ability to create the illusion of separation from Being, through the mind, so as to observe himself as Being. So the masculine is Spirit, the direction of Being. He is life itself, its protector, and also its destroyer. When out of alignment, the masculine, through the mind disengages from Shakti… from feeling and creative energy. He becomes numb and destructive—a separate, lost, limited form unaware of itself as Being.

Masculine and feminine are always One, yet the world of physical reality creates the illusion of duality. Men and women are equally masculine and feminine, Shiva and Shakti, in the highest sense. Only as we move ever further into density...into the mind and physical reality as something separate from Spirit, do such distinctions become in any way significant.

You can find out more about **Maya Yonika** on her website at: www.ramamaya.com

Surrendering to the Feminine

By Charusila

In many of the men I have worked on, one of the deepest wounds they hold is the grief and pain around the subjugation of the feminine that they have participated in, in past lives and sometimes in the current life. Deep in the heart of the masculine is a desire to be consumed by the feminine. The feminine is the container—sexually the man enters INTO the woman, the sperm enters INTO the egg, the masculine exists within the feminine for the first nine months of existence. Out of fear of this desire and perhaps due to a simple lack of awareness, the masculine has historically perceived that it FORCES entry, that it is all-powerful because it can overpower and demand entry. The incredible pain that exists in the heart of the masculine is the deep underlying dissatisfaction of knowing that to really be received by the feminine, the masculine must be invited in. Perhaps it can physically enter—but the entry into the sacred inner chamber of the heart of the feminine is granted only to those who seek it humbly, respectfully and reverentially.

From what I have seen, the masculine feels this pain and, out of fear of this pain, turns away, thereby continuing to deny the feminine. It takes a strong heart to face this grief, face the pain of the collective masculine and in a sense apologize for the ignorance that has allowed this wounding of the feminine, which ensures that almost every woman keeps her inner sanctuary safe and secure beneath the charade of the perfect manicure or the dinner on the table. What choice do we have when our hearts and bodies have been broken so many times by the blind, fearful masculine which chooses to cover its ignorance and fear with brute force and subjugation?

Whenever I work with men and this theme comes up, I see how deeply beneficial it is for both the masculine and the feminine to take down these habitual roles, behaviors, habits and fears and meet each other truly naked. How can the dominant masculine come to deeply honor and recognize his desire to be contained by the feminine? How can the feminine come out of centuries of subjugation to step into the power and strength of universal motherhood that is the essence of every woman? These are deep and powerful themes for a couple to acknowledge and connect with, that will rock every sense of identity they hold dear. What bravery and courage will we have to bring to the surface of our minds in order to take this journey together? And yet, how can humanity survive if this journey is not undertaken, if these questions are not asked?

Perhaps this article is mostly written for men, to alert them to the themes that may be underlying their inability to truly find the feminine. But in truth it will take as much courage from the feminine as it does from the masculine. Despite our nature of yielding, we are so tightly wound in our protection of our own divinity that we often miss it even in ourselves. I would entreat the masculine, if he is truly sincere in his desire to uncover the sacred feminine, to begin this journey alone. Even if you are in partnership, do not declare immediately your intentions and expect your partner to open simply because you desire it.

Be radically truthful with yourself. Are you really, deeply available for this most important journey? Are you willing to meet your own fear, brutality, longing, mistrust? Are you prepared to discover the true power of the feminine? Are you ready and willing to unleash that powerful presence in your partner/friend/daughter for the good of all women? Are you prepared for the changes that may come in your interpersonal dynamic, or the challenges that may come from the other men in your life who get a subtle sense of what you are doing and feel threatened or critical? If the deepest answer in you is YES then I honor you, for you are truly a man. And in your manhood, you will begin to uncover a mystery so sacred it has been lost to the world for millennia.

The fact of the matter is, the Divine Feminine, the Goddess that you may be seeking to come into contact with is actually within you. What we as humanity are lacking is this innermost connection with ourselves. As you come into contact with the Goddess within you, you will subtly be giving permission to all of the women (and men!) around you, to come into contact with the Goddess within them. This is a powerful place to stand. Humanity can truly shift from the choices of one human being.

The Divine Feminine within everybody holds a tremendous amount of power. In Hindu mythology, the feminine is designated as creation, the masculine as the detached, underlying consciousness. We cannot have one without the other. But the subjugation of the feminine essence for eons is coming close to destroying this incredible creation that we are all a unique and magnificent part of. This journey is not simply a personal one. The need for it to be made is much bigger, and the power that is calling for you to step into is not limited to your small, personal mind/emotions/desires.

If the essence of the masculine is logical, linear, rational and controlled, the essence of the feminine is wild, free, uncontainable power. The invitation of this journey from control to freedom is surrender… But to what might you surrender to, and what must be surrendered? In truth, we are not surrendering to anything outside of ourselves. It is not an external force, not a limited notion of just doing what your partner asks you to do, or a controlling and punishing "God" figure that we have to give our power and autonomy away to. Instead, we are surrendering to our own essence, the pure consciousness that animates all of creation.

What has happened, through the length of human history, is that we have built up so many veils, masks and limiting concepts about who we are that we miss the bright, shining light in the center of each and every human heart. So what we are surrendering is these veils, masks and limiting concepts. We're giving away all the clinging and attachment to specialness, separation, being right, even being safe! We're coming to a reckoning with life that magically and radically alters both the relationship with ourselves and every other relationship that creates our life. Suddenly, we don't need theories of how to relate because we simply look inside and find out how we would truly like to be treated. When we give up the notion that the Divine Feminine is somehow separate from what we already are, there is nowhere to go to build a relationship with it.

I am not interested in giving you a list of what women want, or how to treat us. I know that you actually know already. It's just a matter of having the courage to step into what you know, to step into what you truly are. Instead, I want to offer you some basic, simple practices that can easily be incorporated into daily life so that you are not only setting an intention, but actively doing something every day to reinforce that commitment within yourself.

When we set a powerful intention for ourselves, we create an anchor that is capable of holding us through the storms that may come as we start diving deeper. Remind yourself daily of your intention. That way, if challenges come, you will easily remember the reason they have shown up and find the courage and strength to meet them with love and gratitude, knowing that they are the crucible in which our emotional garbage is being burnt off. This journey may not always be enjoyable or easy. But the joy and peace of being that arises from an ever-deepening connection with ourselves and with the heart of mystery that lies within each of us, takes us to a level of fulfilment, one that few have touched.

Here are some practical things you can actually do to help you on your own quest for the Goddess:

1) Make a connection for yourself with a form of the Goddess that you feel drawn to, choose a Goddess image that you can develop a relationship with, and invite Her to teach you. This may be an idol of a traditional deity such as Mother Mary, Lakshmi, Brigid, Kali, etc. Or you may choose a natural object to represent mother nature or even an image that reminds you of the formless, all-powerful feminine. Whatever you choose, allow it to be something that speaks to your heart, and is pleasing to your eyes. And ideally, choose something which doesn't simply excite your passions, because you are attempting to cultivate a relationship that goes beyond the hormonal. And we all know how hard it is to really pay attention when we're feeling sexually driven.

Once you have chosen a form to relate to, take some private time to speak or write or sit and meditate with the image and communicate your intentions. Be as clear as you can and become humble enough to ask for help. Ask the Goddess to teach you, and be willing to listen to the messages you are given. You may want to get a journal to keep with the image, that you can write your intentions and questions into, as well as record any insights or answers that you receive. This is a gentle, daily process and you will reap great rewards with the input of only a few minutes of focused attention every day. It will also help you to keep your intentions present to yourself, especially in the moments when more challenging emotions or experiences come to the surface. Your intention will form an anchor that keeps you present in the moment and allows you to trust in the process.

2) If you feel comfortable and safe with the women in your life, ask them to share their experience of the Divine Feminine with you—and REALLY listen to them. Do not listen to disprove, to be right, to figure it out, to get a specific outcome. Instead, listen more with the heart than with the mind. Learn to listen to what is beneath and between the words. Listen so that the woman you are listening to knows that she is being heard.

3) Make a commitment to uplifting at least one woman in your life, without telling her that you are doing it. This may be your partner, your daughter, a woman you work with or even a cashier at the supermarket. Make choices in your communication with this woman that are about increasing her sense of self-worth, giving her a positive experience of herself every day, supporting her to know that she has value and unlimited potential. If it is someone close to you, take active steps to facilitate her actually getting to experience those qualities in herself, and being able to make choices that take her closer to self-actualization—for example, supporting her to take a class in something that she is inspired by, or encouraging her to express her creativity or explore her spirituality. Start to taste the beauty that you get to experience in yourself when you know that the twinkle you see in her eyes is there because of the choices you made. And beyond that, receive the gifts that she shares with you willingly as she grows into being able to receive your unconditional love and support.

4) Choose one trait/habit that you know does not serve the feminine in your life, and really pay attention to yourself. Whenever you see yourself play it out, take a moment to find out what the trigger was. For most of us, it's something to do with our sense of self-importance/self-worth being compromised or challenged. When we feel threatened or insecure, we tend to lash out (verbally, emotionally, physically) or withdraw. The feminine is very sensitive to these movements, even though they may not be able to communicate how they know. When you investigate yourself, you will probably find that the knee-jerk reaction automatically releases and you become available and open once again.

The thing about women is, even when they don't realize it or actively acknowledge it to themselves, they are incredibly intuitive, especially when it comes to friendship and relationship. This is why simply making a declaration about your intentions means little. The women in your life will feel it when you make a change, and they will respond even if it's never talked about consciously. Suddenly you will find them sharing more of themselves with you, or reaching out to you in deeper ways. You may find them getting stronger and being more assertive, as they sense that they are really, finally, being seen and heard for all that they are.

Revel in this shift, for it is a gift that reminds you that the work you are doing with yourself is really paying off. Acknowledge these women for what they are sharing with you, or the ways in which you see them growing. Let them know that you see the shifts and that you honor and appreciate them. There may be emotional wobbles, as they learn to be comfortable stepping into the next level of their own power and authority. Do not be afraid of these wobbles, as they are actually proof that the woman is growing and blossoming. Give them space, support and encouragement. Fight for the biggest vision you have for the true expression of the Divine Feminine in their life, and gently remind them that it's always darkest just before dawn!

For myself, as a woman, because I have been taught that it's dangerous and inappropriate for a woman to be powerful, whenever I am challenged by life to take another step towards truly expressing myself and owning all the gifts I have been given, I tend to get very scared and very small for a couple of days, and a lot of old emotions come to the surface. At this time, all that I need is for the men (and women) in my life, to see that I am afraid and give me space to accept that, while fighting for my bigness. The more that I receive the reflection from the important people in my life that they know that I am big enough to face this challenge, and that they are on my side, the quicker I find the courage to step in. Of course, as soon as I step in, everyone else around me benefits, because I have even more to give and greater wisdom to share. So it's a win-win situation!

When I'm emotional, the best thing I can be given is just a loving, open space in which to feel my emotions without judgment or resentment. When there's no resistance to emotional energy, it actually moves through pretty quickly, and frees up a lot of awareness in the process, that had been suppressed by the idea that I was somehow wrong or lacking. It's amazing what a little bit of unconditional love can do for a woman. We have been judged and misrepresented for our emotionality for so long, that when someone simply chooses to sit with it and allow it to be and see us in our wholeness, not limit us to that transitory emotion which we're experiencing at the time…then we shift very quickly, and profound growth comes along with it!

In short, when you allow a woman to simply be who she is, then you will find that beneath all of those things that men subconsciously fear—our emotions, our pain, our insecurities, our true sexual potential, our power, our mirroring of men's own shortcomings back to them—is a deep and potent love that is just waiting to be uncovered and allowed to shine freely.

Charusila is a healer and teacher who works internationally inspiring people to come closer to their own authentic nature, through individual and group healing, workshops and writings. You can find out more about her at: www.charusila.com and www.facebook.com/divinelightenergyhealing

Full Circle

By Navneet Kaur

Princes and Damsels

Once upon a golden time... I was a little girl, raised in the bosom of a loving family, tucked into bed at night with a teddy bear, a fairy tale, a kiss and an unspoken promise that life at home would always be this kind to me. I would dream in vivid color, surreal scenes, swirling and merging stories, painted images of the princes and damsels, dragons and slayers, heroes and villains that had been scorched into my brain whilst listening, eyes closed, to the story being told by the parents and grandparents I trusted so.

At that tender age I had a knowing of the interconnectedness of life. I would sit in my Grandma's garden, close my eyes and feel the breeze, the rain, the sunlight, whatever there was to feel, and it would touch my soul. I would smell the freshness of the grass, the blossom on the trees, the musty scent of the soil and know I was in touch with Earth as a living, breathing Being. Eyes still closed, listening to the cars in the distance, to the wind in the trees, to birdsong, and eventually picking out the tiny noises of insects busy in the ground tending to their lives, I would feel connected to all of life and sense a sacredness, a Godliness in all things.

In those first few years of life, I flowed relatively freely. I believe now that I was in touch with my divinity, my Goddess. All that time ago, relishing the changes in the weather and dancing my dance of joy or anger or still calmness or rage, embracing the relevant mood in connection with nature and the essence of life, I flowed with my inner tide.

I bumbled my way through the tussles of teenage years,

exploring the depths of sexual encounters with the naive eyes and mind of a cotton-wool-wrapped novice. And I had lots of fun doing so, albeit fringed with guilt and shame passed onto me by my lovingly protective and Catholic-raised family. My mind imprinted with the fairy tales of my younger days, I fully expected all my encounters to lead me to my prince, the savior with whom I would share my life, who would be there for me at all times to offer protection, security and love; who would rescue me at a moment's glance from the scrapes I was bound to have, being the meek and tender damsel I believed that I was. It took only two kisses of two frogs, then the third such union turned out to be with my prince. At sweet seventeen I met the man I was to marry (at twenty) and share a not-so-sweet eight years of confusing marriage with.

The interactions and events that touched my life from my youth into my thirties lent themselves nicely to the formation, or perhaps strengthening of my inner masculine essence. David Deida in his book *Blue Truth* describes it as building layers. We have our core sexual essence, usually either predominantly masculine or feminine, occasionally neutral. And depending on what we are exposed to or how we perceive events in our lives, we begin to build up layers around our core.

At one point in my youth, desiring a better connection with and approval from my dad, I joined his cycling club. And although it didn't truly bring me closer to him, I was accepted whole-heartedly by the younger members, and swiftly became "one of the lads". I learned that to remain flowing, expressive and passionate in the company of young men was dangerous, as they really didn't know how to handle emotional energy; so it lead to rejection or an angry rebuke. I responded by striving to be more like them, coarse and sarcastic in humor and tough on the outside, though the exterior belied the sensitive interior. The Goddess was stifled!

I can see, looking back, how the migration from my true self caused me to make inappropriate choices in many areas of life, especially in my relationships with men. And I know that this contributed extensively to the lack of success in my marriage, and to the relationship following it. This story, however, is not intended to be a dissection and analysis of a "failed" relationship (or two or three) inflicted on an unsuspecting reader; but rather, a sharing of the lessons my experiences delivered to my door, with the hope that something useful might be gleaned by others. It would be a wonderful thing if by reading this, others were protected from having as many "successful break-ups" as I've had. But oftentimes, first-hand experience is really the only way to grow... the sweetest flowers grow in the deepest dirt, do they not?

Grow up!

The experiences that transpired in my marriage propelled me swiftly into the arms of the next man; which in turn, after a much shorter time filled with more intense experiences, propelled me firmly into life as a single woman—on the edge of breakdown, but determined enough to find my way through things for the sake of my daughter. I embarked on a journey of healing and personal growth, and opened myself up to exploring the spiritual aspects of my nature. The Goddess, however, at this point, was still sleeping soundly.

What I began to see, as I unfolded my creases and learned to stand tall, was the illusion of expectations and the falsehood of a need-soaked love. For the first time, I was able to see that the fantasy of what my prince would be to me, was born out of a sense of incompleteness. I had been searching for the one who would be able to fill the gaps of my jigsaw puzzle of a life and make me feel whole—a romantic concept expressed in so many love songs and poems... *Please, please, make me whole again!* What a huge expectation to lay at another's feet, especially someone who is also painfully aware of their own insufficiency. It was time to grow up and take responsibility for my own healing and wholeness.

My first lesson in truly accepting self-responsibility came as quite a shock. I was pouring my heart out to a beautiful matriarchal healer, sobbing heavily as I recounted the times my husband had attempted to rape me, fully expecting a tea and sympathy reaction, the kind of well-intended response that helps to keep a person rooted in victimhood. Instead, with nothing but love and genuine compassion burning in her eyes, my healer asked:

"And what was your part in this, my dear? What did you do to create this situation for yourself?"

Pardon??? I was stunned into silence for a little while, which gave this gifted lady a chance to gently explain to me the realities of life: We all play our part in creating our environment, our circumstances and the reactions, whether cold castigation or loving affection, we receive from others. My marriage had been filled with insidious abuse, looks of repulsion, softly spoken but brutal put-downs, and simmering resentments which left no room for tenderness or lovemaking. I used to pray that he would hit me, form a bruise, do something that was obvious to others, or that was at least beyond the limits anyone would expect me to endure. My prayers were answered!

At that point, sitting there with my healer, I took responsibility for my part in the events, and something amazing happened... Suddenly, I felt stronger. Accepting self-responsibility, and also knowing who and what we are *not* responsible for, are sure steps towards becoming self-empowered. We know we are empowered when we no longer feel any need or desire to inflict control or power over another person. We are empowered when we feel self-sufficient and complete, exactly as we are.

On a practical, foundational level, this manifests in being able to look after ourselves and our family; to earn a living, pay the bills, keep a warm home and a supply of food and essentials for the household. On an emotional level, it involves dropping neediness in favor of accepting that we can easily fulfill our own emotional needs by practicing self-love and self-nurturing. And from this place we can form loving relationships with everyone in our lives—not just one singled-out, obligated hero.

Eyes Wide Open

When we find our wholeness from within, we no longer search for missing pieces. We accept that we are whole, even though we still have more to learn about ourselves, more to heal. Our wounds don't make us incomplete. They are simply a part of our journey. It is in learning how to heal that we learn how to be at peace with our imperfections. In fact, it is our very imperfections that create a perfect human experience. Discovering this level of self-acceptance enables us to accept those around us as they are, too, seeing beyond their sore-spots and wound-driven behavior to the real beauty of their soul.

The veil is lifted. We see people for who they are in a real way, without projecting our dreams and therefore expectations on them. We see with clear eyes the ego games at play, the fear-born manipulation and lies, and we can choose to play along or else to walk away, so long as we take responsibility for that choice and the outcome. With such clear sight we learn to trust ourselves, to be confident in our ability to discern what feels appropriate for us and what needs to be passed by. We develop gut feeling, intuition. Or rather, we realize that we always had good intuition and now we are taking the next step by having the courage to follow it. A natural consequence to this is the melting of our need to put our trust in others. When we say "I trust you" without first having developed the ability to trust ourselves, those precious words carry an undercurrent of forceful expectation: "I trust you… but you'd better not let me down, or else!" Removing the need to trust another removes the potential to be thrown into the pit of yucky, gut-wrenching, heart-breaking despair when they do the human thing and...*let us down*.

Open up

During the learning process, I seemed to form a protective cast-iron coating, dropping the softness I associated with dependency in favor of the cool hardness of independence. This impacted strongly on the partner I had at the time, with my harsh refusal to accept his help (his method of demonstrating his love for me), leaving him feeling redundant and emasculated. Needless to say, that relationship didn't last.

I buried the soft feminine along with the Goddess under a cloak of masculine energy. In my eagerness to drop neediness, and my desire to be a self-sufficient, strong and reliable mother for my daughter, I had allowed the *yang* in me to take over. It served its purpose; and life for mother and child was stable and safe. I had proved I could survive and endure. But is this what life is truly about? Enduring… survival? And how was I to fit a loving relationship with a partner into this framework?

It seems to me the task set for many modern-day women is to learn how to fully embrace their femininity, their softness and vulnerability—and yet refrain from entering a submissive, self-defeating feeling of worthlessness while out in the patriarchal, competitive and often aggressive modern world. And conversely, how to refrain from becoming masculine, or raising our yang energy to the point beyond balance, in order to deal with life and those challenges we encounter along the way. How do we gently stay centered in our sense of feminine empowerment, and avoid the pendulum-swing extremes of submission, and aggression?

I cannot claim to be able to answer this question in full. I am still very much a student in this field. Yet I feel that the ability to do this must be in part linked to our ability to be open. When we are relaxed, feeling secure and comfortable, our nature is to be open, honest and accepting, centered in the flow of heart energy. When fear strikes, when we feel threatened, unsure or exposed, there is a tendency to close. The heart center constricts, our energy withdraws, we become judgmental of ourselves and of others. If, at that first recognition of constriction and closure we instead breathe into it, gently encouraging our energy to expand, to allow ourselves time to feel centered and connected once more, then we can stay open—open to exploring all aspects of our own nature, the creative giver, the warrior princess, the delicate flower, the multitude of glorious, if somewhat confusing facets of ourselves… Open to the Goddess within in all her forms… Open to receiving the qualities and gifts a man is able to bring into our lives when we allow him… Honoring his inner God as much as we desire him to honor our inner Goddess, as we each respect our differences and recognize the absolute preciousness of those differences… And open to the idea of surrendering our false competitiveness in order to create an energy exchange in which the feminine and masculine are able to merge safely into one another.

It is far too easy to distort the energy exchange by altering the roles we play in reaction to one another's ego games, manipulation and drama—switching from the original roles of mutual lovers, to parent/child, abuser/victim, wounded/healer, teacher/student and many other combinations of opposites. Before we know it, the relationship has become one-sided and unbalanced. It steadily gathers resentments as it moves into co-dependence, and ultimately towards breakdown.

In a prolonged, healthy relationship, there will be a natural level of growth and evolution, with each person teaching and healing the other, inspiring and supporting them on their journey. This occurs as a result of joint explorations of love and life, of facing challenges together and of rejoicing in the joy of living together—not by forced adoption of false, ego-based role-playing. A sacred spiritual evolution of souls within the framework of human relationship is allowed to transpire, by learning how to love without need, without enforcing obligation, and with the knowledge that compatibility is the natural consequence to acceptance. And it seems to me that the establishment of such a respectful and divine relationship cannot but help assist a woman to reconnect with her inner Goddess, or a man with his inner God. This level of relationship is in fact the journey to the Goddess/God, and the path to surrendering ego to the service of soul.

Surrender

An empowered, real-love relationship personifies an interdependence that is established based on soul-yearning (a natural and primordial energy flow), yet allows each person to remain an individual. To put this concept in a more poetic frame: while the sun and the moon exist perfectly well of their own accord, each a complete and beautiful creation in their own right, they can't fully experience themselves or their own existence without the interaction of the other. The sun's fire burns too brightly for him to see himself clearly. So he needs the reflective surface of the moon in order to see his true potential, and to be inspired to burn even brighter. The moon's beauty and grace is hidden in the dark until the light of the sun falls on her, and permits her a radiant glow.

Acceptance and understanding of this natural interdependence brings true humbleness and unhindered union to relationships between lovers. It involves a surrendering of the Goddess's chaos into the steadiness of the God, and requires the patience and stability of the God as he holds the space, whilst the Goddess unleashes her wildness. Both man and woman, God and Goddess must delve within to their core selves to find the courage and trust needed to allow themselves to let go of themselves, for the sake of one another.

I feel it is only possible to truly embrace the above concept after creating a firm foundation of independence, self-empowerment and self-sufficiency. Until then, the primordial soul-yearning is distorted into ego neediness. And it is this that takes us into unhealthy, co-dependent relationships. Even when there has been a development in awareness, and co-dependence has been recognized as the illusion that it is—and perhaps especially during the phase where effort is being put into establishing independence and strength—the sun/moon analogy could feel wrong and threatening because of echoes of co-dependence and determination to never feel needy again. But when self-sufficiency has been mastered, it becomes easy to accept.

Self-sufficiency, independence, empowerment—all of these things allow individual survival. When the soul/human has lived this way for a while, it begins to feel its yearning again because our incarnations aren't about just basic survival. They are about richness of experience. And while life can be experienced as an individual, I believe the soul won't be fully content until it is truly seeing itself reflected in the glow of its complimentary partner, as are the sun and the moon.

I am not quite forty. But I can feel my life beginning anew. I am back in the land of Princes and Damsels—only now they are Kings and Queens. Wiser and stronger through experience, yet stripped of the layers and outer shells, I re-enter the innocence and vulnerability of youth, feeling every nuance of man's energy as acutely as a newborn's skin feels the touch of its mother. I spend time in Mother Earth's garden and savor the connection with nature and my primordial Self. I have awakened the Goddess. Or at least, I've shaken her enough to stir her from her slumbers. She is still sleepy, and needs teasing from her resting place—a little gentle persuasion for her to fully lift all of her faces to greet the sun. Though I know I am capable of striding through life as my individual self, I believe the blossoming of my true nature will occur more so if the excursion is enriched by my union with, and my surrendering into, the God-ness of man. And just maybe, that union will be good for him, too.

Part 3:

The Yang Perspective

Feel Something, Man!

By Anonymous

In one sense, it's really quite simple: women just want to be loved. The problem, I suppose, is that love itself is complicated. It isn't something that is simply on or off, black or white, you love someone or you don't. Love is multi-faceted, embodying different feelings, colors, shades, depths, qualities, intensities, intentions. A man might "think" that he loves a woman. But then the woman doesn't "feel" it. Because love, really, isn't a thought at all; it's a feeling. The thought is a step in the right direction, the same way that stepping out of your front door gets you partway to the grocery store. But stepping out of the door doesn't equal arriving at your destination.

Women want to be loved FULLY. The way that most men love women is like a tease. It's like blowing someone a kiss, when they want to feel your lips against theirs. It's like leaving them a note, when they want to hear you whispering in their ear. It's like brushing your hand across a woman's thigh, but never getting around to making love. They get a sense, a hint, a taste of what they want. But then they never quite actually get it. They are left in a state of being half full, half empty, never completely satisfied.

It really comes back to that notion of feeling. Yes, it's not a manly word. Feeling is a sensitive, vulnerable, squishy thing, associated with weakness and not being in control, pretty much the antithesis of machismo. The one place that men are most likely to feel something is in their penis. And that's a great place to start, if nowhere else. Women want sexual, physical satisfaction, same as men. But they also want much more than that.

Feeling isn't just a physical thing, of course. Feeling runs the gamut from physical pleasure to pain, from anger to sadness, from affection to annoyance, from desire to repulsion, from fear to love. You can look at a woman, your girlfriend or wife, or a woman you just met in a bar and think, "Man, she is so f*$@ing hot. I definitely want to get close to her, feel her out, give her some good loving." And the woman may pick up on this attraction, and even be thinking just the same things.

But meanwhile, there's more going on within a woman. On the surface, there is the realm of thoughts, up in the head somewhere, rattling around the brain, same as us guys. And then there are feelings, which are somewhere else, a different concept entirely. Really, they're everywhere else. They're all throughout the body, in every limb and appendage, in every cell. And they aren't experienced just physically. You can feel anger, and it can then manifest in your stomach or your back or your feet, as a physical sensation. But the source was non-physical. Where did the anger come from? Feelings are somewhere you can't really pinpoint. They're just in a person's soul somewhere, connected to and mixed up with thoughts within the mind, as well as connected to the body. But they are also somewhere beyond that, in a different universe almost.

In order for men to connect deeper with women, they need to connect with these feelings within themselves. Sounds cheesy I know, too airy-fairy, not very masculine, feminine essentially, not grounded in the real world. But get this: it isn't about tossing out your manhood. It isn't a matter of not being a man, of not being strong, the provider, of being an active force in the world. It isn't about flipping everything around and becoming feminine or something, as you let women take over being masculine. It isn't even a matter of evening things out so that women and men are the same, equally masculine and feminine, yin and yang, essentially the same but with a few different body parts. No, that isn't the way to go.

It isn't about losing something: your masculinity, your strength, your power, your abilities to make things happen, to fix that which is broken, to bring home the bacon, to impress your woman and give her confidence that she is protected and taken care of. It isn't a matter of losing some part of yourself. It's a matter of finding yet another part of yourself. It's about connecting with the subtler realm of feelings, emotions, intuition, sensitivity and love. But it isn't an either/or kind of situation. You can have both. You can be a man, and you can also feel something, beyond just the pleasurable sensations in a good hard-on. Connecting with the feminine within doesn't mean you lose your masculine identity. Instead, you gain something. You gain what is necessary to connect with women at their level, in their realm, playing their game, loving them where and how they want to be loved, deep in their hearts and souls. And you open up a whole new world in the process.

Connecting with what is going on deeper in your soul is a multi-dimensional process. There are a million ways to approach it. If you are in a relationship with a woman, then that provides a great opportunity to discover some more stuff going on in that weird realm of feelings, simply by changing your focus and your intentions. The typical dynamic is that men keep women at a certain amount of distance. Women are always trying to pull the man closer, and the man is perpetually saying, "Hold up there honey, that's just about enough right there, let's not get carried away."

Like I said, what most women really want is for the man to love them fully. But men more often only want to love women partially. Obviously, it isn't quite as simple as that. A man can sometimes be deeper in love with a woman than she is with him. I've certainly been there before. But more often, it's the woman who wants to experience a deeper love… and the man doesn't know what the heck she's talking about.

So in your relationship, just make a decision, a choice, an intention that you're going to take things to another level, because you're ready for things to be a little more interesting.

How that might play out, exactly, is anybody's guess. There are, of course, the usual things that you can *do*, such as telling her you love her every day, buying her flowers more often, taking her out to a romantic dinner, buying her new lingerie, greeting her naked one evening as she comes home from work and leading her into your bedroom of moody music and lighting and scattered rose petals, etc.

Those are all good ideas, of course, and certainly worth doing. Your woman will no doubt appreciate such gestures. But in all honesty, that's just scratching the surface. And get this: in a sense, ***it's actually missing the point***. Because, you see, that's the man taking the male approach, which is *doing* something. That's focusing on the world *out there* somewhere, rather than the world *within*. Doing things can be an expression of that inner world, of course. Sending flowers to your woman's workplace with a note attached can be something that lets your woman know how much you love her. But keep in mind: *it isn't a substitute for love*.

Love, that which is the real stuff of any relationship, isn't in flowers or gifts or nice words or deeds or rose petals. It's within you, and within her. Much more important than any outer actions on your part, is how you make her feel on a day-to-day, hour-to-hour, minute-by-minute basis. Much more important than what you do for her or even say to her… is simply how you look at her; how you feel about her; how much you value the relationship; how much attention you give to her; how intently you listen to her; how much you value her words, her ideas, her perspective; how much you honor her feelings, whatever they might be; how much you respect her; how much you consider her an equal partner in your relationship.

Focusing on these things is much more important than ever giving her a gift, because this is what any relationship actually consists of. And you can give her all of these things every minute of every day. Or at least, you can give them to her more often than you presently do. And *that* will make a real change: in you, in her, and in the love that flows back and forth between both of you in your relationship.

Now, taking this approach, making the intention to connect in a deeper way with your woman and honor her to a greater extent for who she is, will most likely result in some stuff going on that you hadn't anticipated. It will stir up some things in her, and it will stir up some things in you. Yeah, you might end up feeling some more feelings. Oh man, now what??

This is where the real chance to make some inner changes comes in. The trick is simply to not do what men generally do when it comes to feelings: ignore them, deny them, snuff them out, pretend they don't exist. Instead, take a look at them, acknowledge them, and then let them be a part of who you are, part of your being, part of your masculinity and your manhood. Connect with them, instead of disconnecting from them. Because in so doing, you can connect with that deeper, more subtle place of feeling in general, which is where love resides. When you are more connected with that place of feeling and love, then you open up another world within, create a new space that your relationship can grow into, and then you can really take things to a whole new level… And isn't it really the most manly thing that there is, to truly love a woman?

There's another way to change things within and connect to that deeper world inside your soul, which you can do whether or not you are in a relationship. Again, it starts with a basic intention: to simply start noticing what's going on. Just as if you pay more attention to your woman, then you'll start to see a lot more going on within her than you realized was there; by paying more attention to yourself and what you're experiencing in your mind, and beyond that within the realm of feelings, you'll start to see that there's a lot more going on than you ever realized. You will begin to see that the assortment of constant thoughts and subtler feelings and emotions that are hovering around you, moving in and out of yourself, nagging at you or even tormenting you at times, are actually just tips of much larger icebergs. And you can follow these leads down to access reservoirs of energy, feeling, emotion, creative juice, passion and love that you hadn't realized was available to you.

Now, I didn't mean to completely knock "doing things" before. We live in physical bodies in the physical world. Our relationships are inevitably about doing things for one another, and we should be mindful of what we do for each other as well. I was simply making a point that if you focus entirely on the doing, while neglecting the *being*, then you'll miss the boat, so to speak, in terms of figuring out how to connect deeper with women. Because in the most basic sense, men are doers, and women are be-ers (no, not beers, though some men might prefer it!). Of course, we are all both doers and be-ers to some extent. But it's a matter of what we tend to focus on. And in order to make that greater connection with women, men need to start focusing more on being and a little less on doing.

But there are things that you can *do*, which will change how you *be*. The most obvious of these is meditation. One of the main objectives of meditation is to start noticing more what is going on inside of you in terms of thoughts and feelings. In a sense, meditation is both an exercise you do, and also something you don't do. Because the ultimate goal is actually to *not* think. But in this case, not doing something isn't such an easy task. However, I'll refrain from giving a complete lesson on meditation and leave that to the experts. There are a million and one resources in that department these days, from books to movies, workshops, meditation clubs, information online, etc.

But that is one important and very accessible way to start changing your *being*. Because connecting in a real way with women requires changing more than simply what you do in an outer sense. It demands changing and evolving yourself, going deeper into your mind, heart and soul, and in so doing shifting the idea of who you are, what manhood really is, what womanhood really is, what love is, what a real relationship is… so that men and women can finally start seeing eye to eye. It does mean, to some extent, men gaining some more femininity, as well as women gaining some more masculinity. And both men and women will find that this is a natural thing, when they allow it to happen, because we all have some element of masculine and feminine qualities within us already.

So, let's combine everything mentioned here, as well as add the element of sexuality into a straightforward exercise that involves doing, being, meditation, the penis, feelings, and awakening your sexual potential. They say that statistics have shown 98% of men masturbate—and the remaining 2% are liars. So, assuming you're one of the more honest 98%, here's a lesson in masturbation that can be very powerful.

Again, it starts with a basic shift of intention. Instead of doing it hunched over a magazine or staring into a computer, turn it into a spiritual and meditative exercise. Sit cross-legged and naked on the floor, the bed, wherever works. Have some music playing if you prefer, or do it in silence. Close the eyes, or else leave them open if you like, and simply bring your attention into your body, all of it. Become more body conscious, more physically aware. There is a catch here though: don't actually stimulate yourself, yet.

Bring your attention to your second *chakra* (spiritual energy center in the spinal column), the sexual chakra, located in the region of the genitals. But for now, simply keep your hands resting on the knees, or assuming a *mudra* (hand symbols with different spiritual meanings, you can look them up online).

The idea here is, for one, to take self-pleasuring and sexuality in general and make it something spiritual, sacred, valuable beyond just getting off or relieving tension. And the other purpose of the exercise is to start tapping into your sexual energy from *within*, rather than focusing on the outer by stimulating the penis to bring about arousal. This can actually result in suppressing sexual energy, because you can end up trying to force something when the energy behind it isn't really there. You might get a hard-on and be able to ejaculate; but you don't actually tap into the real energy, the full potential that exists for sexual feeling and that sense of connectedness that it can bring.

So just meditate on, or simply contemplate your own being and whatever is going on within the multiple levels of yourself: physically, mentally, emotionally and spiritually. They are all actually connected in some way, and they can all tie into sexual energy. Sexuality is, most obviously of course, a physical act. But it is also a mental act: you think various thoughts about your partner, about yourself, about whether you're enjoying it or not enjoying it, about how attractive you find the other person, etc. It is an emotional act: you feel certain things, not just physical pleasure but non-physical feelings of love, desire, horniness, primal passion, oneness with another, etc. And then, it is also a spiritual act: the joining of two bodies into one, and two souls into one, that ultimately can produce another human being.

So the idea is to not stimulate yourself, until the sexual feelings and arousal are already there. Tap into the root of the energy itself first, before connecting with it physically. Allow the feelings to come into your awareness, focusing your attention on them without trying to force anything to happen. If this leads to arousal, an erection, then just let it happen. If you find that you can sit there in cross-legged meditation with a full hard-on without having touched yourself, then consider yourself a lucky man. Your sexual energy is definitely intact.

However, if you feel that you need some stimulation, then go for it. But wait until you're feeling the sexual feelings first, and your body is responding at least to some extent with an erection, before stimulating it further. Perhaps that won't happen at all at first. In that case, just sit there, paying attention to whatever is happening, just allowing your energy to awaken wherever it is able to. Eventually, it will lead to sexual awakening and arousal, if that is your intention. But you don't *force* it. Instead, *allow* it. There is a subtle but crucial difference between the two. It may take some time for the true depths of your sexual energy to surface on its own—maybe after a few days of trying this exercise, maybe weeks, maybe months. Because most of us, men and women, haven't properly handled our sexual energy. This exercise will give you the opportunity to balance and direct your sexual energy in a whole new way. (Incidentally, for any women who might be reading this, of course you can do the exact same exercise with the same focus and intentions.)

So let's say that you find yourself at that point where you're fully aroused. There are a couple of different directions you can go with it. One is to remain in a non-doing meditative state, keep your hands on your knees or elsewhere, and simply allow your manhood to stay erect, while focusing on allowing the sexual energy to flow.

You will find that it isn't a constant, static thing, this flow of energy. It will lessen and then it will increase. But very likely, what will happen as you tap further into your sexual potential, is the energy levels will look something like the Dow Jones Industrial Average during a bull market. The sexual energy will increase to some extent, and then decrease a little. Then it will increase some more, to a point greater than before. Then it will, yet again, decrease and retreat a little. And then it will come back stronger than before, finding a new high. And this can go on pretty much indefinitely, so that the energy and the feelings keep getting stronger and stronger. If you are able to stay erect and just allow this to happen on their own, then you can find yourself entering some very intense, powerful, wondrous states of being, by allowing the sexual energy to simply be, rather than manipulating and forcing it, and then expelling it quickly through ejaculation.

The other option, if you feel like you need some further input or else you just want to heighten the intensity, is to go ahead and stimulate yourself, while staying seated in cross-legged position. The same thing will happen as described above, most likely intensified. Just pay attention to whether you're forcing things, or simply enhancing that sexual energy that is already there. In this case, though, you will of course have to pay more attention to the possibility of climax and ejaculation—which is an important thing to start focusing on and working on controlling anyway.

The easiest way for men to lose their sexual energy is by ejaculating too quickly. As soon as you do so, your sexual potency takes a huge nosedive, and it takes time for it to come back. Many men are conditioned to think that getting an erection means you have to ejaculate. But in fact, you can allow yourself to get completely aroused, totally erect, hard as a rock, just shy of the point of ejaculation, maintain that state for a certain amount of time… and then allow yourself to go flaccid eventually, and then carry on with the rest of your day, without ever having ejaculated.

What happens is that you then *retain* that sexual energy and potential within you, instead of releasing it through ejaculating. That doesn't mean that men should never ejaculate, by any means. Instead, it's a matter of building the sexual energy within you, so that it continues to heighten and intensify. For one thing, it will result in having greater control over when you ejaculate, so that you can last longer in bed with a woman. And also, this building of the tension and retaining your sexual energy can lead to much deeper experiences of pleasure, bliss and ecstasy, as well as stronger, more powerful orgasms and even altered states of consciousness. But again, I'll leave descriptions of how exactly to achieve those extremes to the experts in various books and teachings.

For the time being, you can simply use this basic tool of tapping into your sexual potential, and see where it leads. For one, it can be an avenue for connecting much more with some of those feelings and emotions that men tend to be disconnected from. By turning sexuality into a spiritual experience, instead of primarily a physical one, you can start becoming more aware of some of those icebergs beneath the surface of your consciousness, and start increasing your awareness of more subtle parts of yourself within; because awakening your sexual feelings and energy will in turn awaken other parts of yourself that are buried beneath the surface.

Of course, there are a multitude of other tools available for increasing one's self-awareness and connection to the subtle realms within, especially in our modern-day world of mixing cultures. Beyond countless different strains of meditation, and a vast assortment of spiritual teachings to choose from, there's yoga, tai-chi, tantric teachings and techniques, tribal trance dance, rebirthing, reiki, sweat lodge ceremonies, couples workshops, emotional body workshops and all sorts of other weird-sounding and interesting possibilities. You can do all of those things and more.

But the two most important things that you can do are simply to pay attention to what is going on within yourself and pay special attention to your woman. Combined with your simple intention to create a new level of relating in your romantic relationship with a woman, these commitments have the power to take your relationship to levels and places and worlds of love, pleasure and spiritual meaning that you hadn't imagined could exist. And as a man, there is no journey more interesting, more exciting, more challenging or more important than learning how to love a woman fully and completely.

When I Get What I NEED Instead of What I WANT

By Martin Hannon

Around eight years ago, I took my first Tantra weekend workshop. By then, I had figured out that I wanted to try something new. I had done relationship in a certain way which led to predictable and ultimately unsatisfactory outcomes. I wanted something different, and felt this workshop would get me there.

During the workshop, I was unexpectedly "cracked open." I felt as if I had been hit with a sledge hammer and then run over by a truck. I was oozing messily out and into the world around me. It was not pretty. I had lost some semblance of my masculine control (gasp!) and I was far from being comfortable. I had been taken out of my head and put into my body where I saw and experienced much of the shame and hurt I had, for so many years, skillfully stuffed way down into the deepest darkness of myself, just so I could cope. I have since come to realize that in life, I had been merely surviving… instead of thriving.

The brochure that had advertised this weekend workshop used fun sounding words like "embracing, releasing, opening, discovering, breathing and dancing." Yet I was feeling vulnerable, fearful and quiet… words not used in the brochure and words that, at that time, would not have typically been used to describe me.

I did not ask for this. I didn't sign up for this. Nobody *warned* me. Even though I had done other "personal work" and the man who told me about this workshop was someone I trusted, I was still quite shaken.

Many in the group with whom I shared this weekend

appeared to have fared better than I. At the end of the workshop, we were encouraged by the facilitators to continue the practice that we had been given, which was intended to support each of us as we progressed. We also had the roster of participants and were encouraged to follow up with each other in the interest of building community. An opportunity to sign up for the more advanced classes was also offered.

This is one situation where I got what I *needed* and not necessarily what I wanted. What I *wanted* was the good food, the hot women and the massage (which my friend had told me about) and I didn't mind some "dancing, releasing and opening" to go along with getting what I wanted! However, what I *needed* was to witness, in the course of having an actual, in-my-body experience, how being shut down, controlling and tight was getting in the way of being my authentic self.

Here was an opportunity, cleverly disguised as dis-ease and discomfort, to see that I was getting exactly what I needed. And while this was happening, there was a safe space created by the facilitators and participants to "hold" not only me, but the few others that were also challenged.

Throughout my life, I was always one to direct and to control in order to get what I wanted. However, I have realized that when I am open, quiet and in the moment, something new then has a chance to reveal itself. To release that drive to get what I want takes courage. It takes surrender. I acknowledge that courage within myself and especially in those around me. Through others, I can see how it is done when they show up unafraid and, even when they are afraid, their will and determination serves as an example for me when I am less than hearty.

Getting what I need can feel anywhere between terrific and terrible. It also has a way of having no boundaries. **Getting what I want has *limitations*.** I can see that getting what I want is usually time-limited, requiring further control or tightness in order to get more. **Getting what I need is *boundless*** and I am not the only one who benefits. I have a strong personality. I can affect what happens around me and to others. The experience of having expectations (being focused on what I want), is remarkably different than just showing up open and available to getting what is needed.

{Caveat: This applies best when in interpersonal relationships and NOT in the business world, where there exists a whole other mindset that absolutely requires direction, focus and planning toward achieving results that must accomplished in order to... *fill in the blank.*}

Interestingly enough, in my zeal to get what I want, I am admitting that I do not trust that there is another force in motion that has what I need... just for me and just when I need it. What happened in that first workshop was exactly what I needed. I only got as much as I could handle… and yet it was excruciating. But through the challenge of the undoing of my old patterns and ways of being, I came out on the other side softer, more open, less controlling and as a result found that my ability to do relationship was improved.

Also, getting what I want is mainly a mental process. I have to be in my head to discriminate and discern all the input that quantifies, qualifies and justifies the pieces of evidence I use to see if I am ultimately getting what I want (I'm getting a headache just thinking about this). And guess what? While in my head, exercising my superior mental masturbation skills, I am not in my body. (In a much lesser moment so many years ago, I was told I "could analyze a grain of salt"… that stung!)

In that overly analytical mode of being, I am not truly present in the moment. I am missing out on the cues, subtleties, nuances and signals that my body is experiencing. The way my body feels the rush and flow of vibrating aliveness is missed when I am in my head. My lover will miss out on the possibility of gifting me her energy and love, and also receiving mine, if I am trapped in my head wondering if I am getting what I want instead of being open (surrendering) to what is needed for the connection to be rich, lustrous, invigorating and rewarding.

These tantra workshops have a way of showing me a lot... consistently! Even today, I know I am in the undoing when my stomach starts to hurt, when my throat begins to tighten and my heart begins to ache as the energetic blocks that are holding me back from fully expressing myself are shifted, released or dissipated. This is what the tantric breathing exercises, the movement and the meditation are designed to work on. Certainly, these are experiences I would not *want*. During those uncomfortable or even painful points, I can choose to make the workshop itself wrong, and complain that I am not getting what I want. Or I can just breathe deeper, and trust that I am getting exactly what I **need**.

The Men's Tantra Circles that I help facilitate (see menstantracircle.blogspot.com) is a place where men get what they need. Often they arrive with one thing to explore because they have figured out that they want something. Fair enough. I get that. Then they find out there is more. In a safe and sacred space, men get to leave behind what no longer serves them, which is often what is holding them back from experiencing the simplicity of getting what they need.

As the founder of the Men's Tantra Circle, which meets twice weekly in Los Angeles, **Martin Hannon** moves through every aspect of his life with a sense of pride and masculinity that has been all but lost in our culture today. His presence serves as an inspiration for the potential of all men. One of the greatest issues in relationship today is that modern men and women have been taught to neutralize their "charge"—to become more alike and "get along smoothly". Martin fearlessly invites and guides men to rediscover what it truly is to be a man, and from that place walk authentically in the world and experience the magnificence of Woman. Over the last ten years, Martin has studied Tantra with Bodhi Avinasha, Dawn Cartwright, Rundy Duphiney and Bernie Prior. Furthermore, he has done extensive work and study around re-discovering man's true role in life and relationship with the Men's Division International, where he defined himself as a leader among men. He is also deeply passionate about loving his woman Charu, founder of Embody Tantra, and sharing the wisdom they are discovering together with the world. Check out what Martin offers at: www.MensTantra Circle.com

Now That I've Found Her, What if I Lose Her?

Marion Doerflinger

I've been thinking long and hard on this essay that I am attempting to write. I have made many attempts, and deleted them all. The reason for all this spinning in circles is because I have been avoiding writing about the one issue in my personal quest for the Goddess that bothers me most—now that I've found her, what if I lose her?

After thousands of wasted words, I have finally surrendered to this thought that demands my attention, my best effort as a writer. I'm going to write simply about what would become of me if I lost my Goddess.

This is a great, although mostly unspoken, fear of mine because I had never been so happy for so long until I found my Goddess. I'm not used to such a long stretch of unbroken happiness. Now that I've found her, what if I lose her?

I'd never spoken so confidently nor carried myself with such strength before I found the Goddess. Now that I've found her, what if I lose her?

It seems to me that every man starts out his life with a vision of the perfect lover, the lover who will make him complete. He sets out like a knight in search of his queen, he braves many pitfalls and sorrows. He goes down many wrong roads. Some give up hope.

But I found my queen, my Goddess. I have found what every man seeks. And now that I have found her, feelings of unworthiness fill my mind in my weaker moments and ask me how I can possibly expect her to stay, for this to be forever, when I am so unworthy, so common?

What will become of me if I lose her?

This question surely haunts every man who seeks his Goddess, and it surely discourages many from ever setting out on that great, noble quest. How can I stand to be this happy if there is no assurance that it will last forever; if I can't know for sure that I will never lose her?

I tell myself not to be so needy. I throw around modern words like co-dependency in my discussions with myself. I even tell myself I'll be fine, that I'll regain my feet and even love again.

And I suppose I will. But it will only be after a time of grief, out of which I will emerge an older, hopefully wiser man. But that man will lack the flame that the man I am now carries. He may be deep water, but he will not be triumphant fire.

I discussed these feelings with my Goddess after having basically given up on ever writing this piece. She quoted some ancient wisdom—"To be far is to have the hope of being near. To be near is to have the fear of being far."

I thought on this wise saying. I saw that when you are lonely and unhappy, the hope of finding your one true loves keeps you going. I also saw that, when you have found your one true love, the fear of losing her keeps you from being completely happy.

I am sorry if my words dampen the spirits of he who seeks his Goddess. But the Goddess quest is not a thing to be taken lightly. Only those who have calculated the risks ought to set out on the journey. Finding your Goddess is akin to rolling the dice. And heartbreak is the price you pay when the numbers go against you.

Ah! Deep breath. Let it in. Let it out. Relax. Clear the mind. Think. Write the conclusion.

The above is a gloomy and sad thought that kept persisting on being written until I finally gave it a voice. And now that I have given it a voice, I find that within my very question (now that I've found her, what if I lose her?) lies the answer.

The Goddess, once found, can never be lost, even if the mortal container in which she has chosen to abide while she reveals herself to you, goes away. For it is true that you never found the Goddess. She didn't need finding. She was always with you, always within you.

You did not need to find her after all. But you did need to *see* her for the first time. And she showed herself to you, after much long searching, through the eyes of your lover.

And, with this cheerful thought, breaks the dawn. What if I lose her? What if the lover through whom I was finally able to see the Goddess goes away?

I will stand. I will be alright. Because what my lover brought to me is eternal, even if she should someday find greener pastures. Her words… Her touch… Her love… The depth of her understanding. All these things will live on in my mind and memory and I shall count all the good memories, as a miser counts his gold coins, all the days of my life.

And what is going away anyway? It is a slight break in the stream of eternity. In that place where the stars play hide and seek and God teaches Her children in pure spirit, my lover and I shall find each other and enjoy the company again and again. You can never lose what you love, for loving her makes you one with her, and she shall always seek you out and surprise you with a golden kiss at an unexpected moment.

In putting these words down I faced and resolved my one great fear since finding my Goddess: that someday I would lose her and then be lost myself. But I have come to see something in the few moments that this writing has taken. What I have been experiencing as the pain of fear, I can now appreciate as the excitement of the adventure of living.

Marion Doerflinger is a freelance writer who lives in Columbia, Missouri. His recently published children's book *Daydreaming Daisy* (co-authored with Josephine Kei Lux) may be seen at BarnesandNobel.com and Amazon.com. He has two adult novels under agency contract with a prominent literary agent in California. Marion may be contacted at: mdpoetryman@yahoo.com. He wishes to express gratitude to Nirtana Goodman for help and advice in writing his essay.

What Women Want Is…

By Francis Eliot

I'm going to tell you what women want. But first, I'm going to say a bit about last night. Last night, I screwed up. My partner was feeling that I was not strong enough, and the worst thing about it was that I could not stay present for her. I didn't give her the sense that she was OK in her feelings. So I couldn't "hold the space" for her to come back to feeling good again. She quite rightly asked me to leave, and I felt abandoned. I was caught up in myself. I was worried that she would never open to me again. I was worried so much about myself that I could not really see her. I could not be present for her. What women want is for men to be present for them, for men to see them, to witness their beauty and mystery, even when they are fearful or angry.

A great healing did emerge for me, later on, and I spent some hours releasing deep and old fears and anxieties. I'd felt abandoned, and only later recognized that the feeling had little to do with the present situation with my partner, who had simply been aware of where I lacked strength and presence. I had let her down by trying to argue against her feelings, and by not initially allowing her space alone when she asked for it. I wanted to redeem myself by being present in her presence. But it was too late at that point, and I was not recognizing that being present for someone does not necessarily mean being in the same physical place as them.

Thank heavens we are now back in love. But it was a strong reminder of the tantric teaching that in the relationship of polarity, it is the masculine who must steer the ship on the feminine ocean. The ocean (the feminine) can get wild and windy; in fact, in its essence it is really just pure energy. If the masculine loses control of the ship, or simply fails to steer, things will not be good!

Many men are too busy trying to justify themselves against women who do not feel truly met. I have been there many times. But men need to ask themselves this: *"Would you rather be right, or would you rather be close?"* I know what I would choose. So I aim to let go of my defenses and remain present when I'm with my partner, steering the ship, not losing my balance and getting caught in stormy waters. Women will test men. They will test their presence.

Polarity

In order for a relationship to be sexy, perhaps even ecstatic, polarity must be present. Whoever takes on the masculine role (this could be a man or a woman, in either a same-sex or heterosexual relationship) must show presence and power. He (or she) should know his mission and live by it. If he is not really aware of his life purpose and task, the one who takes on the feminine role will not feel safe to open. And if the feminine does not open, she will not be living her deepest calling, which is to fully receive herself, as love itself.

Men, beware... she may well be upset by this. It is up to the man to do what he can to be present, even when she is upset, so that she can surrender into her feminine nature. Deep down, most women want to open to the point that they feel they have become love itself. But they cannot until they feel totally safe. And a man busy in his thoughts, obsessed by his plans, constantly doing things, is not safe territory. And nor is a man who does not know where he is going in life, or what his deepest calling is. A man should not expect a woman to open fully into love if he is not fully present and living his mission.

That's a lot of hard work and discipline for men! So, what then is a woman's responsibility in the relationship? If it is a man's responsibility to be present, it is a woman's responsibility to cultivate her desire for the man. Man cannot do this for her. All he can do if the relationship loses vitality is return to the masculine (not wanting anything, just living his life mission and cultivating presence) so that she can return to the feminine (yearning for love). When this happens, the polarity and its associated juice will return to the relationship.

What to do

The Mankind Project (MKP) is an excellent men's work organization empowering men to seek and live by their mission. During my initiation weekend I literally saw men's lives transform. Something happens when men come together without women (and without alcohol or drugs). There is an honesty and understanding that comes, perhaps from not having to keep up appearances or impress anyone.

Men may also seek to solidify and expand their presence by practicing sitting meditation, by focusing their attention on something other than their thoughts; by connecting with something bigger such as Universal Consciousness or the Spirit of All Things; by connecting with the part of himself that was never born and never dies. I myself regularly visit the woods, alone, trusting in a Greater Spirit of which I am a part, doing what I can to connect with the river, the trees, the earth, the air, the stars. Being in my thoughts does not allow me this connection; so I use my movement, breath and sound to help me connect. Just two hours a week makes an enormous difference to my level of presence in the world.

It is also important that a man learns to express presence through the body, through movement, as well as breath and sound. A man may have the presence of the Buddha; but if his body is tight and unable to express physically his honoring, his care, his appreciation of a woman, then she will not be satisfied. In my eyes, he needs to dance! His hips need to loosen, and his attention needs to come down from the thinking head, into the "animal" body.

What men want

What men want is to be valued. I don't think we're looking for much. But even the smallest amount can make a great deal of difference to a man. Primarily, however, we men need to get this value from within ourselves, or from a "band of brothers". Otherwise, we will be so craving it from a woman that we will be unable to see her beauty, which is what she needs. And if she does not get what she needs, then there is little chance of her seeing and expressing value in the man. Then we are in a horrible, vicious circle from which there is only one way out... courage.

Courage

Relationship is a two-way street. It's no good just waiting and waiting... the man waiting to be valued, the woman waiting for her beauty to be honored. If both of you wait, your loving relationship will die. Someone has to make the move. The two of you need to courageously come together with the intent to surrender to loving the other, even if you do not want to be lovers with them in that moment. The ego does not like this. It wants to be right, and it will try its hardest to keep you separated from love. You have a choice to either be courageous, or let the relationship dry up.

As soon as a man makes love to a woman, he activates her resistance to love. At first, she may only be aware of her surrender to love. But in time, it's very likely that her resistance to love will also be activated. As my dear friend and teacher Leigh Tolson told me recently, "Love shines its light on where we are lacking in love". And when the woman is activated, she in turn might just activate the man's abandonment issues. We need to see when this happens. And we need to learn to truly say "ouch" to our partner, without blame. A true "ouch" has no blame, and in this blameless state we become lovable. And then our partner will love us.

Perhaps we will love each other so genuinely that we set each other free. And from this place we might choose to make love for nothing but the pure enjoyment of it. We no longer need anything from each other, because our reconciliation completely surrendered us into the simplicity of being.

Acceptance

It's no good if either of us just keep on being hurt, however. In truth, we need to make the effort to stop telling each other what to do and who to be. We must accept that we are not the same as each other, and we must stop trying to make others into who we think we are, even if this pattern is addictive. We're only doing this so that we do not feel the emotions that arise when we see a characteristic in another that we have not yet learned to accept in ourselves. Certainly, if we can learn to accept each other as we are and not how we want each other to be, then we can get on with living a creative life. Haven't we all had enough of trying to be who we are not?!

Let us focus on what is there, what is in front of us, not what is missing. This goes for how we see ourselves and how we see our beloved (not that there's much difference). And if we feel that our partner is the one who is only focusing on what is missing, are we in fact just focusing on what is missing in our partner's seeing?

We need to take responsibility for our own seeing, and not react to another's. If they do not see us, we let them know, we say "ouch", we clear the pain. And then you might share with your partner how you really felt. You are not sharing this to change them, blame them, make them see or understand anything. If these are your motivations, believe me, it will not work. You are simply sharing in order to share. You are simply showing your heart to your partner. You will know whether you are blaming, because your partner will react, or close up.

Of course there are times when we must say "no", stake out the boundaries. And it is essential that we do so. It may be that our partner is being dishonest, or has fallen into an old pattern of irresponsibility or laziness. But this is a "no" that comes very much from the present moment, and is very different from the more cloudy sense of wanting someone to be different from who they are.

Ritual

So please, let's come together. Let's look into each other's eyes and both say: "I'm sorry for all the times you have felt pain because of what I have said or done". And then let us honor each other. The man places his hand on his heart and courageously appreciates and speaks of the beauty in the woman. The woman puts her hand on her belly and speaks of her appreciation of his value—perhaps not so much in terms of what he has done, but instead more of who he is, who he is to her, who he is in the world.

If this honoring ritual is impossible because of the emotional charge, then you have a choice. Either you decide that your partner is not worth it, and that you made a mistake getting together with them in the first place; so you close down, break the other's heart and dishonor your own.... OR you clear the emotions that are in the way of your seeing the essence of the fellow human being who sits before you.

Do whatever you need to do to get through those emotional blockages. Beat a pillow. Do one of Osho's emotional release exercises; or else EFT; or Byron Katie work; or Ho'oponopono. Do whatever it takes to release what stands between your heart and this other fellow human being's heart. When you do this, you will see that the one who sits before you is the mirror of you. You may see that there is no separation between the two of you. You will love them and you will love yourself—just as when you hurt or hate them, you will hurt or hate yourself. Perhaps we are all with the person we are with, in each moment, whoever they might be, in order to learn how to love. And if we truly, courageously commit to learning how to love, then we will one day be able to set each other free.

Francis Eliot, from West Yorkshire, U.K, is a healer and life-coach specializing in transformation of behavior and consciousness through methods such as bio-energy healing, 5 Rhythms dance, tantra and raw/living foods. He has completed many trainings and studied with various teachers and meditators including Thich Nhat Hanh, Gabrielle Roth & Byron Katie. He has taught Gabrielle Roth's 5 Rhythms since 2004 and is deeply inspired by the healing power of dance. He is also an active father. You can book a personal consultation with Francis, or read his blog at: www.returntoinnocence.org.uk

Pussy Power!

By Anonymous

I realize that some women don't prefer the word *pussy* to be used in referring to their womanhood. And if that's the case, then a man should, of course, go with whatever word a woman wants you to use, be it vagina, vulva, yoni, womanhood, flower, etc. But I happen to like it. For one thing, it beats a lot of the other words out there, which I won't bother mentioning because they definitely don't have a particularly respectful ring to them. And respecting a woman is paramount, every part of her. So I use the word with the greatest of respect and adoration for a woman's most private part.

But also, a pussy is a cat. And a woman's pussy and a cat actually have a lot in common. For one, they're both hairy. They both like to be petted. And when petted they both are likely to start purring (or moaning, in the case of a woman, close enough). They're both sensual, and like to feel good. They're both flexible. Neither of them likes to be rubbed the wrong way. A cat has nine lives, and a woman can give birth to nine lives, or even more… I think you get the point. So for the sake of this essay, if you don't mind, I'll stick with pussy.

A man's cock and a woman's pussy have, of course, quite different roles and energies. The cock is penetrating. Its power is in moving forward, making things happen, getting a woman to open and respond. The pussy is the opposite. Its power is in the energy of attraction instead of forward movement, and of either opening, or choosing not to open. But though the pussy is an important part of a woman, and represents the nature of a woman to open and receive, the pussy isn't everything. It's actually just the beginning. The big mistake that men make when it comes to entering a woman, is that they think, "Well, I'm in. I've succeeded. She's opened to me. I fucked her. My mission is accomplished, the pussy has been conquered. Add another tally to the score."

But get this, guys: this may be true on the physical level. But if you think that sex is all about the physical, then you're completely missing out on the best part. The physical act of sex feels good, of course. But it's only one part of the equation, a small part. There are also the mental, emotional and spiritual elements, all of which tie into sex. And if you haven't explored them to their fullest extent as they relate to a woman, then you haven't gotten nearly as close to her as you thought you did. Simply having sex with a woman and then thinking you've succeeded in getting to know her intimately, is like thinking you've broken into Fort Knox and the gold is as good as yours, just because you managed to get over the fence on the outside. You've got a long, long ways to go still to get to the gold. And you won't get there without the right key, because it's waaaaay too heavily guarded.

A woman's pussy is like a portal, or a tunnel, to the rest of her. But getting into her pussy doesn't equal having made the journey much deeper into her heart and her soul. That requires much more than brute force or even cunning charm. It requires being much more of a man than that. There's a choice that men need to make in their relationships with women, and I'll present that basic choice in a series of questions:

* Are you going to focus on your own pleasure, or are you going to focus on hers?
* Are you going to focus on getting what you want from a woman, or are you going to open yourself up to what she has to offer?
* Are you going to tell a woman everything you think you know, or are you going to learn something from her?

* Are you just going to talk, or are you going to listen?
* Are you going to keep telling yourself that you're "the man", "the best", or are you going to admit that you could stand to improve and become a better man?
* Are you going to use various tactics to convince her to open up to you, or are you going to wait for her to open to you eventually, because she truly, deeply wants to?

Now you might be asking yourself, among other things: "Why should I focus on her pleasure instead of my own? Isn't my pleasure as important as hers? And shouldn't she focus on her own pleasure, and leave me to focus on mine?"

In a word: no.

You've got the penis. The penis is the active element in all this. You're the one making the moves, and the woman is responding to them. You're doing the fucking, and the woman is the one getting fucked. (I use the word "fucked" here in a positive sense, as in "being made love to", but that's a longer and clunkier way of saying it. Same as the word pussy, I'm using it in an intended respectful and fun way here.) Of course, the woman can take charge, get on top and take charge too, but more often it's the man on top doing the screwing, and the woman enjoying getting screwed (hopefully, at least).

So the man does his thing, and the woman is either thrilled by it or isn't. If she isn't, then depending on the quality of your relationship, maybe she'll let you know that it isn't really doing that much for her, and maybe she won't. More often, she won't. So the man gets his rocks off, the woman enjoys it to whatever extent she enjoys it, and then, once the man ejaculates, that's pretty much the end of it. The man gets satisfied almost invariably because it's easy enough for him to cum and get his release, and then maybe the woman orgasms as well and maybe she doesn't. And if she doesn't, then perhaps she fakes it so that the man feels like he's a real man who can satisfy his woman.

So, you see why the man needs to focus on the woman's pleasure? Because the man has more power over their shared sexual experience, by the simple nature of his physiology. Basically, his power in this regard comes from the ability to cut things short, and then be fine with it, while the woman is left hot, bothered and totally unsatisfied. That's nothing to be proud of here in the slightest, guys. It's just reality. And if this is the way it works out, you can be assured of one thing: you completely missed the boat. Maybe you got off, blew your load, accomplished the goal that you had in mind for yourself... but you got nowhere near the buried treasure.

A woman's sexual power for the most part comes in response to the man's active sexual role, be it in a sensitive, subtle way, or (more likely) not so subtle. Partly this is simply because it's the woman's nature to be responsive. And then partly it's also because women don't want to open up until they really feel safe, even if it is their natural response to open up. For example, she may be totally turned on and horny and want to have wild sex with you. But even so she will still hold much of herself back until you've taken the time, said the right things and done the right things to show that you're trustworthy and that you're going to stay present with her if she does open up further.

If all this sounds too confusing and complicating and you just want to get laid and leave it at that—then fine, go for it, it's your life to live as you choose. But if you want to discover the true sexual ecstasy that women have to offer, if you want to get within sight of the gold hidden deep inside of them, and maybe get a taste or a whiff or even a piece of it, then you've got to take on the confusing, complicating challenge of truly winning a woman's heart and her trust.

So here's one practical step you can take that can make a big difference for both you and your woman. When you're making love with your woman (or fucking or screwing or getting wild or engaging in tantric ecstasy, whatever you happen to call it), try this: ask her how you're doing, and how she's enjoying it. But don't leave it there. Because unless you already have an amazingly healthy and balanced relationship that encompasses brutal honesty, she'll almost certainly tell you that you're doing a great job and she's loving it, whether or not that's necessarily the case. Instead, follow it up with "Be honest, I'm open to any pointers, I mean it." And then *do* actually mean it. Because if you don't, she'll probably sense that and you won't get back real honesty, because she won't want to hurt your feelings and bruise your ego.

In order to really mean it when you ask this question, you have to actually be prepared to hear something other than: "You're awesome, I'm loving it, yes, more, you're the man, you're the best". Because she might just take you up on your offer and tell you: "Well, it's not the absolute *best* I've ever had", or even worse: "Not so great, actually".

But if that's the case, whether you know it now or not, do you really want to keep making love to your woman in such a way that she isn't actually enjoying it all that much, or at least as much as she could be? Or are you ready to take a chance, possibly take a hit to your ego, and in the process take a step towards becoming a better man, and a better lover?

Unless you already have a perfectly balanced, fine tuned, truly loving, totally open and honest relationship with your girlfriend or wife or lover, it's going to take some concerted effort on your part as the man, a genuine intention to start moving the relationship in the right direction, towards her inner chamber of buried treasure and bars of gold, which is her real sexual potential.

A woman's true sexual power is a vast reservoir of amazingly beautiful, blissful, orgasmic, loving, embracing energy. But unlike a man's, which is hanging out there in the wind, literally, for everyone to see, and standing strong and proud when it's ready to go, her power is carried within her and is much harder to assess, and access, than a man's.

Getting to this place in a woman requires patience, persistence, strength of character, honesty, integrity, courage, the willingness to admit when you're wrong, humility, playfulness, knowing your own body, a sense of humor, some charm, intelligence, knowledge and experience. In other words—it requires all of the qualities that a woman most desires in a man. And you can't fake it or force your way in. You must have the right keys to unlock her inner doorways. Basically, what it comes down to is being able to sense the subtleties of a woman's energy in any given moment, and to respond and act accordingly. Yes, it's complicated, and it isn't easy. But it is a quest that is well worth pursuing, and one that will be met with unparalleled rewards once you find your way to that which you seek.

So be a man. Take a chance. Take a good, hard look in the mirror. Be prepared to come up against the idea that you aren't quite as totally and completely awesome and amazing as you think you are. This is a necessary notion to lose if you want to discover the *true* power of your woman's pussy, which is her deeply orgasmic sexual nature. Finding that place in a woman isn't something most men are ever going to get remotely close to.

I imagine most men are quite surprised when they hear the statistics showing how many women actually fake their orgasms. And of course, we all immediately assume it's happening to some other unlucky dude. But women wouldn't be faking their orgasms so much—and they wouldn't be able to *get away* with faking their orgasms—if men were more genuinely in touch with their women. But most men just want to hear that they're doing a great job, and leave it at that.

If you're a man who wants something more than that, who wants to unlock the secret chambers within a woman and find that deeper essence of intensely loving embrace and overflowing orgasmic ecstasy, then consider that you've just been handed one of the keys. The key is to *seek honesty from your woman*, about what she wants and what you can do to truly satisfy her. And then be prepared to learn something from her about yourself when she actually *is* honest with you. This simple intention and action on your part can open up a whole new paradigm in your relationship that can lead to an entirely new dimension of loving, and to the real love, beauty and power of the pussy.

On Being Worshipped

By e.b. sarver

When it comes to religion and gods, I don't believe in them. I do, however, find many of the metaphors and techniques within them to be useful. One metaphor I have found of particular value is to hold someone else as either a God or Goddess—to hold another in that space of an object of worship, devotion and adoration. Additionally, being held in this light by another person can be an incredibly empowering and enlightening experience.

It is rare to experience utter devotion and adoration in our lives. In fact, I would guess that most people have never had the experience. I had never experienced it myself until my late twenties, when I became involved with learning techniques of Tantra. I had never truly given it to another until I began to practice Tantra with a partner.

"Devotion frees." ~ Vigyan Bhairav Tantra

Devotion not only frees the devoted, it also frees the object of devotion, or the action one devotes oneself to. Devotion frees through love. To be devoted, truly and wholly, one must first surrender to one's love. This experience in itself is freeing, and is only amplified by the acts of devotion that follow it.

One ritual commonly practiced in modern western neo-Tantra is a massage and bath ritual. The practitioner, or teacher, or guide (whatever word you may choose is fine), acts as a devotee of the God or Goddess whom he or she serves. The receiver, or student, or guided one, is held as the God or Goddess, and simply receives the devoted actions of the teacher.

I'll offer one man's perspective of being treated like a God, and what that experience did for me, how it changed me, how it altered my perspective toward women, and how it altered my life…

It was and is one of the most enlivening experiences in my life and memories; to have a beautiful woman hold that kind of space for me, kneel down next to the tub and bathe me gently. She coaxed me to breathe and emote, and to keep eye contact with her. She encouraged me to let go and make the sounds of what I felt in the moment as she devoted herself to caring for me. She looked into me, saw me, and held me as a true manifestation of the whole of masculinity, as a God. She asked me to tone and chant with her, and our voices merged with the sound of the room, filled the space; and our minds and souls seemed to join together, the light of candles and smell of incense expanding like liquid air.

During the experience, I felt feelings as if for the first time. Emotions came powerfully. I could feel them well up and almost seem to overwhelm me… but they never did. I wept from the power of the love I felt. I was able to surrender fully to my emotions in a way I never had before. I felt energy course through me like electricity, enlivening every nerve, and waking me up to a larger truth: that we have within us a divine nature that may be unleashed by being treated as divine.

After the bath, she asked me to step out of the tub. As I reached for a towel, she simply shook her head "No" and took the towel before my hand reached it. She knelt down before me and gently dried my entire body from toe to head, one part at a time, gazing into my eyes for much of the experience. Somehow this drying was even more opening and revealing than the bath itself. I knew in that moment why ancient Jews viewed the washing of feet as such a sacred act. I felt truly upheld as a being of light and of immeasurable power. I felt the strength of masculine love flowing from my center, filling the room, filling her.

It was sexy too, but not in that hard, strong, erect and typically masculine expression of sex. It was sexy in the sense of that deep and eternal current that flows from the archetype of King or Lover: Ahimsa, Agape, the love for mankind, for the Earth, for the whole of life and the universe, the holding of the scepter of action that directs the flow of her divine energy. I had become the thunderbolt. I wept with joy. I weep now as I write this in the remembering of the experience.

> "We are God—took us a long time to figure it out, didn't it? —and it's high time we stopped messing around with all this guilt crap and got down to business, which is, I think, creating Heaven on Earth. Let's affirm our past and say goodbye to it and get to work on the present." ~ Paul Williams, Das Energi

What I learned from this experience is that devotion really does free. In being treated like a God, I truly felt divine. I felt loved, held, understood and accepted in a way I had never felt before. In that experience, I realized the power of holding others in this space. Since then, I have given this experience to a number of women, some as clients in my healing business, and others as lovers or friends. The experience is always profound, for both the giver and the receiver of the devotion.

To devote oneself in such a manner requires a kind of surrender to love and a complete acceptance of the other that we seldom allow ourselves to experience, if at all. We usually approach those we love with a head full of stories about how that person is or is not this or that, how and where that other person is weak or strong, when that person has let us down or held us up, etc. To devote oneself means to let go of all those things, and treat that other person like a divine entity to be worshipped; to surrender oneself to a love that deeply frees one to an authentic expression of love, for true love is without limits, and demands that kind of deep surrender to emotion.

To have someone devote herself to me in that manner freed me to experience a depth of love not just for that one particular woman, but for all women everywhere, in a way I had never experienced before. I am eternally grateful to my healer, who held me as a God and gave me the ability to hold any woman as a Goddess. She healed not only myself in that moment, but also the women I've known since she gave me the experience. She gave me a direct experience of how specifically to transform much of the toxic energy that exists between men and women in our culture: dissolve it through devotion.

If you've never had an experience of being worshipped like this, I cannot recommend it strongly enough. If you've never worshipped someone, I cannot explain how truly freeing it will be when you do. You must experience these things for yourself to truly appreciate them.

e.b. sarver is an author and healer who has been practicing Tantra since 1998, and working as a healer and Tantric guide since 2002. He also uses other healing techniques, including: massage, Reiki, NLP, hypnotherapy, EFT, emotional release and sound healing. He presently resides in the vicinity of Los Angeles, California. You can contact him by email at: tantric.evan@gmail.com

How I Love My Wife

by Sasha Lessin

For most American live-in couples, evenings end with "I'm too tired to make love" according to Newsweek. Twenty percent of America's couples share intercourse less than ten times a year. This "bed death" causes relationship death. But rejoice—the Daily Double Tantra Connects offer an alternative to weakening libido and inevitable break-ups.

Daily double tantra connects

My wife Janet and I make love at least twice—usually three times—a day. We work at home and create our own schedule, so scheduling is easy for us. We recommend that you and your partner make dates to touch souls and genitals twice daily. Here's an idea of how my wife and I structure our day around lovemaking…

3AM: I feel a gentle kiss on the lips. But then I feel tickly whiskers and hear purring and realize it's my cat, Cleo. Cleo wants me to feed her and put her outside to pee. This accomplished, I work at my computer till 7, do yoga till 8, then make breakfast for Janet.

Foreplay from the get-go

I start foreplay—I fix tea, toast and turkey bacon. Then, also foreplay, I hear and help her expand her dreams, twilight imaging and plans for the day. I focus on her, serve her and make her receptive to afternoon lovemaking.

About 10AM, I bike to the beach or gym, swim or lift weights, then pedal home. We eat, talk and shower for our afternoon delight—Honoring the Shakti Shrine, and Embracing the Bucking Bull.

Afternoon delight

I ask Janet if I can undress her. I say what I admire about her body as I disrobe her. I invite her to lie on her back, touch my right palm to her heart and put her right hand on my heart. I rest my left hand on the back of her right side. I say, "Put your left hand on my right side." We gaze deeply into each other's eyes, fully connected to one another.

I say, "I'm delighted to serve you, my Shakti."

I love this pure experience of intimacy. I then say to her: "May my adoration heal any hurts that I, or others have caused you. May our hearts join. Meet me, your devotee, at the Yoni Nadi Shrine. There, together, we transcend our separate sense of self and join the cosmic dance." Then I ask, "What words have you to consecrate the worship I offer?"

Rub her right

I ask her if she would like a massage. She rolls onto her belly and I gently tug her toes, rub her soles and legs, massage her fingers, palms, arms, then back and bottom. I help her turn over onto her back. I keep eye contact with her as I massage her front; first feet, hands, arms and legs. Then I glide my hands over her torso, barely brush labia and nipples and gently massage her belly. I pull her rectus muscles from side to side and trace her ascending, transverse and descending colon clockwise. I massage her face and head. Finally, I stroke and knead the muscles inside the leg (especially the gracilis muscles, where the clitoris roots insert). I press my fingers deeply into the muscles above her pubic bone.

"May I touch your Sexual Shrine?" If she consents, I connect all her chakras with sacred sector energy. I rest my left hand gently on her heart and hold my right hand over her yoni (vulva). I beam love from my eyes into her left eye. We breathe together three times, then I settle my hand gently on her mons and say, "I love you. Feel our hearts connect; energy vibrates between us. I send you love as I breathe out; inhale it." I exhale, draw my navel back toward my spine and up, tighten my pubococcygeal and anal sphincter muscles and imagine energy fountains rushing up my spine from tailbone, through my heart and out my right hand into her yoni.

As I inhale, I feel energy I sent her move through her heart into my left hand. My right hand stays on her yoni, my eyes continue staring into her eyes as I slowly move my left hand to her crown.

"Goddess of Love, I invoke thee and invite thee to enter Janet's crown and move through her central channel to her yoni shrine," I say. Then I move my left hand to her brow chakra. Successively I move my left hand to her throat, belly and rectal chakras. At each point, we take three breaths, continuing to eye gaze and connect with each other energetically.

I say, "I'd like to fondle your drapes and the skin over your pearl."

When she says, "Oh, yes, please," I say: "Make sounds and direct me with words; give me feedback." I gently stroke her outer labia, roll the clitoral hood around but avoid directly touching the crown yet. When her outer vaginal lips swell and reveal the inner lips, I softly trace circles, spirals, horizontals, verticals, diagonals and figure eights on them.

I alternate long, short, inventive, sensitive and playful strokes, softly tap, knead and pinch the hood and labia, then brush the crown.

Polish her pearl, lick her labia, pet her pudentia

When the inner labia is engorged, I ask, "Would you like me to polish your pearl?" (The pearl is the clitoral crown). As we hold our gazes locked together, I blow on her outer genitals, plant baby kisses and twill my tongue round on her crown, lick her labia, flick my tongue into her yoni. My mouth envelops her clitoral hood and, through the hood, my lips stroke her inner clitoris. I salivate generously, lubricating her orifice.

After thirty minutes or so I say, "I'd like to enter your sacred cave with my finger." If she says "Yes", I wet my right ring finger in my mouth and softly touch her vaginal opening and then say, "Pull my finger in." When I feel her vaginal muscles pulse, I ease my finger into her cave. Inside her yoni, I curl my finger toward her navel. The finger rests gently against her sacred sector/G-spot/yoni nadi. We breathe ten breaths together while I imagine my finger extending energy from her yoni to her heart.

With the finger inside her, I trace a light "come here" motion, caressing her G-spot, slowly and softly tracing her cave's inner upper surface from cervix to orifice as I kiss her pearl, lap her labia, wet her with saliva.

I turn my wrist from side to side which moves the finger inside her in a crescent pattern on the urethral sponge atop her yoni ceiling.

After fifteen minutes I ask, "Would you like two fingers inside?" She nods and I curl my right middle and ring fingers together along her yoni's ceiling. I move these fingers up and down the transom over the door and out the yoni, with a "come here" motion, from cervix to orifice. My left hand rests gently on her belly and I press the ring and index fingers of this hand above the pubic bone until I feel my fingers inside pushing to meet my fingers that press her abdomen externally. I create interactive dances between my fingers inside her yoni and the ones outside her belly. I feel her sacred sector swell between the fingers on her abdomen and those in her vagina.

I memorize which internal locations give Janet the greatest pleasure.

Encourage emotion

If, while I'm touching inside her, she tenses, numbs or burns, I say, "Free associate—say whatever comes to you."

She often remembers things that traumatized or closed her down emotionally and sexually. She relives and relates childhood events, past lives, fantasies, abductions, spirit attachments.

She screams, cries, laughs, makes strange sounds. "Let your feelings out, Sweetheart."

I hold her as she sobs and speaks to each person who hurt or neglected her. If she tells me she's angry at me, I say: "Louder. Let me know how mad I make you."

When she's expressed all her emotions, I ask her to fantasize, rewrite and role-play the situation. I ask her to create an affirmation that reinforces the program she'd like to keep for situations that evoke the hurt she has emoted.

I keep my fingers inside on the spot that triggered her catharsis as I enact her parent or lover the way she wished they had been. When she relaxes, I move my fingers back and forth from the area that stimulated the painful memories and into an area that felt good when touched until she enjoys both places.

Enjoy her ejaculation

When Janet recognizes, releases and creates alternative outcomes and we have replaced the trigger areas—areas that initially burned, hurt or felt numb—with memories of pleasure, she orgasms (spasmodically contracts her vagina). I make sounds with her. As she orgasms, she simultaneously ejaculates, dribbles or squirts (a few cubic centimeters to several ounces) divine nectar (amrita)—clear or slightly milky, sweet-tasting, alkaline fluid from her urethra into my mouth. I croon, "You're beautiful," "I love you," "You're coming into your power," and other affirmations.

These affirmations imprint powerfully as she ejaculates. I keep my right hand in her yoni and hold her close. After several minutes, with added lubricant, very carefully (to prevent tearing the now-desiccated tissue), I withdraw my fingers. I lie next to her, holding her tight, my hand on her yoni.

Feel fine with 69, then ride the bucking bull

I lie back and we move into mutual oral-genital loving. Janet turns about, kisses my lips, looks in my eyes, slips my wand into her yoni, rotates and pumps her pelvis around the wand.

I avoid ejaculating. I pull my belly toward my spine then up and tighten pc muscles. When I feel my prostate and seminal vesicles nearing discharge, I hold back, saving my seed for our evening tryst.

(If you don't have time for this full afternoon connect, at least spend fifteen minutes sitting with your legs over each others' hips or lying on one another, gazing in each other's eyes. Let your genitals touch. If you're a man-woman pair, stuff the man's wand into the woman's cave, even if he's limp. If the man has an erection, insert but don't move. That's your preview of coming attractions. Save your energy for evening.)

After our afternoon connect, Janet and I work a few hours, then walk through the woods to the mailbox. I make dinner, we talk and share with one another, then go upstairs.

Bless your evening lovemaking

That evening Janet lies on top of me. We breathe together, then syncopate breath-taking turns, exhaling through the mouth into the other's nostrils, saying "Take in my love, hold it in"; and inhaling, we say "I take in and hold in your love."

I imagine running energy from my perineum, genitals, belly, throat, heart, brow and crown chakras into Janet's. We take three such syncopated breaths for each chakra, blessing each as follows…

We pulse our anal sphincters and say: "I love you. Feel your base and enjoy health, safety and security."

We snuggle our genitals together, saying: "I love you at your genitals, and bless your sensuality, creativity and sexuality."

We touch bellies and say: "I love you in your power chakra; take what's yours."

We rest our right hands on each others' hearts we say: "I send you love from the heart."

With our hands behind each other's necks: "May you speak honestly and sing your true songs."

We join brows and look up into each other's eyes untill they appear to merge, then say: "I celebrate how you understand and intuit."

Finally, we flow energy between our crowns and say: "I merge with you. May you experience unity with the Universe."

Engage in extended lovemaking, employ hand-assisted techniques

After we kiss, twill and play orally with each other's genitals, I lie on my back. Janet sits on my hips and inserts my wand in her yoni. I reach my right hand behind her buttocks and use this hand to direct my wand's angle and stroke in her yoni to rub, churn and tap my wand tip against her favorite internal erotically charged loci.

As her excitement builds, I very gently insert the ring finger of my left hand into her rosebud. I coordinate how I move this finger with the way I use my other hand to move my wand in her yoni. Through the tissue separating the yoni and rectum, I let my finger and wand feel each other and respond together to Janet.

After Janet has had as many orgasms as she wishes and drenched me in amrita, she asks me to roll over on her and release my seed as I look in her eyes. We make ever-louder exclamations, then roar like lions as I squirt. I remain inserted several minutes, then kiss her lips, whisper loving words, invite Cleo the cat onto the bed, then sleep.

Sasha Lessin, Ph.D., Dean of Instruction at the School of Tantra (www.schooloftantra.com certifies professional tantra teachers and trains students and seminar participants how to love each other better. Sasha and wife Janet developed All-Chakra Tantra (www.schooloftantra.net/Store/Books/AllChakraTantra.htm the comprehensive relationship training program that begins with How To Really Love A Woman: 4 Tantric Trysts (www.schooloftantra.net/Store/Books/HowToReallyLoveAWoman.htm

How to "Meet" a Woman

By Martin Hannon

During a tantra workshop for both men and women that my partner Charu held recently, an overriding and difficult to ignore theme was felt and even outright spoken by the women: "We are dying to be met by men!" These women were powerful and vibrant, and were an excellent cross-sectional representation of all women.

Another woman who had read one of my previous blog posts (at MensTantraCircle.Blogspot.com) sometime ago wrote: "We are waiting… we are listening."

These invitations are so obvious…so loud…so insistent!! There is a definite calling out to man from woman, like one of those new huge and very bright multi-changing roadside billboards that are popping up everywhere. You cannot miss one of those billboards. And yet a call from woman, the most valuable of all calls, is apparently being missed.

What many men do not know, or they refuse to rightly acknowledge, is that woman is the most intuitive creature on this planet. Any man who thinks he can successfully bluff his way through any "meeting" of woman is mistaken. Of course, we can all bluff our way through some superficial social or business interaction that is short-lived. But any meaningful interaction that is to exist for a sustained period of time, regardless if it is short term recreational or long term committed, will be explored and questioned through her intuitive realm… Is he being present; is he grounded; does he operate with clarity?

If there is a shred of hope for a true "meeting" of man and woman, man must show up. At the bare minimum, he must *be present*. This is the essence of tantra—**Be Present**. Being grounded in who you are as man, preferably grounded on a foundation of honor, integrity and reverence for woman, is essential to relating with clarity. Having these three things occur in only brief moments just isn't enough. When these qualities are integrated… when we as man do not have to think about them, then we just *are* these qualities, we embody them. Meeting woman from this place then is easy. There are so many women looking for just this. There is a definite calling out to man.

Here is an exercise you can explore while you go about your day. Notice how woman looks at you. She is always watching. Notice how she is listening to you. She is listening too. Are you upset/uneasy that she is watching? On some level, are you afraid to be revealed when your bullshit runs out? Do you feel under the gun? Or do you embrace this watching and listening, because you know that you have nothing to worry about?

If you have nothing to worry about, chances are great that you are present, grounded and clear. Woman cannot help but respond by opening and flowering. She wants to open. When woman feels unsafe to open, to experience the fullness of her destiny, it is akin to a criminal act. When she is allowed to open, because it is safe to do so, and then is truly met by you as a man, it is a gift to you and also to all of mankind.

Following is a letter that illustrates my point, that I received from a lovely woman, Tracy, who passionately and eloquently writes of a recent loving adventure she shared with Larry, one of the men who regularly attends my weekly Men's Tantra Circle groups…

"Together we discovered new heights, new pleasures and never grew weary of the journey. We simply could not get enough of each other. This was the most romantic experience of my life, but also the most sexually fulfilling. I have never wanted someone more, nor felt my partner want me in the same way that I wanted him."

Does that sound like the kind of thing you would like your

woman to say about an experience with you?

Read on for the rest of the story…

* * *

Tracy's Story:

To reconnect again after 33 years makes for an amazing story, especially given the fact that Larry and I were always just friendly acquaintances with a few common threads, having grown up in the same town, attended the same temple and high school. Reunited by Facebook in August, who would have predicted an incredibly romantic weekend together in Scottsdale to be the outcome?

Larry told me about his men's group about a month ago, with some trepidation. Not trepidation on his part of belonging to the group, but in sharing this concept with me and wondering if I would be open to this idea. I'm sure a big part of it was wondering how an independent woman on the east coast would react to this? But after I read through Martin's website and understood the philosophy behind it more clearly, I was thrilled that this man that I was sharing this growing connection with was so willing to search within himself to ultimately become a better man and a better partner. It solidified for me that Larry was a man worth making my own investment in, even with our geographic differences.

As the day of our trip finally approached, I realized that this had been a very different courtship for me. At this juncture we had spent countless hours on the telephone sharing secrets, life experiences, joys and sorrows and simply getting to truly know each other. I knew Larry better before we ever met (again) than any man I have ever been in a relationship with.

For me the day of our meeting finally dawned with an incredibly long plane ride to Phoenix. When the plane landed, late of course, I could hardly breathe. I texted Larry from the ladies room to be certain he was already there, and his simple response was, "Duhhhh!" To which I responded that I was incredibly nervous… and once again a very Larry answer of, "Breathe TK!"

Upon exiting the gate area he was waiting right there and immediately recognized me. We hugged, all still a bit awkward, and went on to get my bags. Another hug, exchanges of "how do I look", and off to the rental car counter.

Finally in our car and ready to begin the adventure, I asked him to kiss me… Promising, but I did not feel the connection that I expected yet.

The ride was smooth and relaxed and we got involved in the process of finding our hotel. Once we arrived at check-in, while I was busily involved in the process, Larry came up behind me, pressed the length of his body against mine as I was leaning against the front desk, and hugged me from behind. That was when the current went off. That was the defining moment that this connection was going to extend to the physical with the most simple of efforts.

Experiences of intimacy are difficult to write about, but in an effort to support Larry's work in your group I must share. At 51, I consider myself a woman of experience. But I have never before found this kind of joy of connections between two people. From that first touch in the hotel lobby to the last bittersweet kiss at the airport, it was perfect. Larry took his time to listen to my signals, to look into my eyes, to wait for my reaction to his touch. Together we discovered new heights, new pleasures and never grew weary of the journey. We were constantly ready to try something new, talk, explain, teach, share, laugh and cry. We simply could not get enough of each other. This was the most romantic experience of my life, but also the most sexually fulfilling. I was respected, cared for, cradled, embraced and touched to my inner core. I have never wanted someone more nor felt my partner want me in the same way that I wanted him.

I was spoiled, satiated and renewed. Most importantly, time stood still.

On our last night in Phoenix, we finally left our own little womb and joined one of my best friends and her husband for dinner at their home. It was hard to escape our own space to do this, but they welcomed Larry and absolutely loved him. As we were leaving, I pointed out a beautiful vase of tiger lilies on the dining room table to Larry, and told him I now understood about Martin's reference to the flower. I let Larry know that I had truly been worshipped to the very core of my flower.

I am not sure that the word thank you is enough to say. But thank you for sharing your lessons with Larry and now with me. I have found a man who completes me, and now I know what true fulfillment can be. We look forward to meeting again and continuing this journey together.

* * *

Can you really afford to wait another moment before you tap into this potential? It's all in the being present, in being grounded and in creating a clear masculine space… just like Larry was holding for Tracy. The tantric techniques and the Core Masculine Principles that I teach each week in the Men's Tantra Circle are the building blocks for creating and living a life of ease, to move authentically in the world, and to experience the magnificence of Woman.

Gabriel Morris is an author, photographer, world traveler, outdoors enthusiast and spiritual seeker, with a B.A. in World Religions. He was born in Vancouver, Canada, raised in rural northern California and has also lived in Alaska, Hawaii, Oregon and Alberta, Canada. He has been traveling the world off and on for more than twenty years, while simultaneously walking a spiritual path of learning and self-discovery. He is author of *Kundalini and the Art of Being* (Station Hill Press, 2008), a gripping spiritual adventure story and hitchhiking travelogue; and of several other books. To see photos and videos of his world travels and read excerpts from his other writing, visit his websites at gabrieltraveler.com & www.kundalini-fire.com.

The contributors, re-listed here in alphabetical order by first name:

Alice Grist is author of *The High Heeled Guide to Enlightenment*, the book that charts Alice's journey from party girl to sassy spiritual woman. Alice is also the author of the forthcoming *The High Heeled Guide to Spiritual Living* (2011). Both books are published by O-Books. Alice is the founder and managing editor of Soul-Café (Soul-Café.net), an online network dedicated to "women who know there is more to life than lipstick". On Soul-Cafe Alice regularly interviews and features the spiritual advice and writings of experts and authors. Soul-Cafe provides a safe, happy space for all spiritual seekers. Alice is also frequent contributor to many magazines and online lifestyle sites, often writing about spirituality in her own quirky, accessible and fierce style. She is a frequent guest on many TV and radio shows. You can also find her on her main website at: web.mac.com/alice-grist/Alice_Grist/Welcome.html

Amanda Lyons is a holistic therapist, facilitator and kundalini yoga teacher with over 20 years of experience in therapy work and a life-long interest in spirituality, particularly in how to use spiritual philosophy as a foundation in all relationships. Amanda offers her services to both men and women with a wide range of needs, yet has found that her work often takes her into the realms of relationships, esteem-building and empowerment. For more information on Amanda and her work please go to: www.angel-sandblossom.co.uk

Anaya Thomas is a Certified Kids Yoga Instructor, C.M.T, Wedding Coordinator and on a strong mission to empower and bring back the Goddess Energy. She is also the creator of The Primal Feminine, a spiritual group and network of Divine

Women and Men that seeks to bring forth the Goddess Movement. Her desire to rebirth the true meaning of rights and freedom as a woman has contributed in helping to heal the imbalance between men and women. Her future goals will include beautiful exotic journeys and ecstatic dances that embrace both feminine and masculine essence in the true honoring of themselves and each other. Please contact her for further details. Facebook: The Primal Feminine, Website: www.meetup.com/The-Primal-Feminine-and-Masculine/ Email: primalfeminine@hotmail.com or info@wigglesngig-glesyoga.com

Andrea Kay O'Loughlin lives in the Midwest of the United States and shares her passion for literature—especially poetry—with her students. Confronted with a life-threatening illness (sarcoidosis), she turned away instinctively from Western medicine, pursuing instead Eastern alternative therapies such as yoga, meditation and massage. Now in remission, she has rediscovered herself, embraced wholeness, seeks mind-body-spirit balance, and only recently has discovered tantric/kundalini energy. She is passionate about life and embraces "extraordinary ordinary" moments. Andrea welcomes questions and dialogue at: akolough@earthlink.net

Asttarte Deva is the founder and owner of Center for Intimacy & Life Enhancement. Asttarte is a relationship coach and offers solutions in sexual issues, spiritual direction or guidance, family problems from the past or present, intimacy fears, phobias or frustrations, solutions for singles and dating, health & wellness concerns and general life problems in the way. She is also a Massage Therapist, Advanced IET Practitioner, Tera-Mei Seichem, Shamballa and Lotus Light Reiki Master, Yoga Teacher, a Certified Melchizedek Priestess, a Holistic Practitioner, Spiritual Shamanic Healer, and Initiated Ancient Egyptian

Goddess. She offers integrated Healing Retreat and Coaching Sessions combining professional coaching, meditation, holistic healing and massage therapy. She is here to express her creative passions, share love with the world and guide you on your journey! She has an ongoing blog at SexBlissLifeCoach.blogspot .com and her main business site is at: IntimacyandLifeEnhance mentCenter.com. She is located outside of Philadelphia, PA and lives with her son.

Barbara Yednak, from Phoeniz, Arizona, is a licensed massage therapist as well as a healing energy channel. She enjoys photography and graphic art and designed the cover art for a recently published book, *The Light Upon My Path*. She is also part of a band called the Desert Winds Steel Orchestra. To watch and enjoy the music go to: www.youtube.com/watch_popup?v=YKWCsY1Da28 You can find Barbara on Facebook at: www.facebook .com/byednak or: www.facebook.com/pages/ HeartSpace-Community/136518193082775?ref=ts For your own personalized Sacred Yoni and/or Lingam art to use in sex magic for manifesting what you desire, contact Barbara at: azhealer@mind spring.com, or go to Yonifaces on Facebook for more information and designs: www.facebook.com/profile.php?id=1000020026867 34&ref=ts#!/profile.php?id=100002002686734&sk=info

Charusila is a healer and teacher who works internationally inspiring people to come closer to their own authentic nature, through individual and group healing, workshops and writings. You can find out more about her at www.charusila.com and www.facebook.com/divinelightenergyhealing

Dashama Konah Gordon, based in both Los Angeles and Miami, is an internationally known teacher, author and lifestyle coach, founder of the Global 30 Day Yoga Challenge, Perfect 10 Lifestyle online community, Yoga for Foster Children, and Pranashama

Yoga Institute. Her powerful message has reached millions of people around the world through video, online and print media. Dashama is a teacher of teachers and travels the world offering yoga certification trainings courses and retreats. You can find out more about her on her websites: www.dashama.com, 30dayyo-gachallenge.com/ and perfect10lifestyle.com/

Elaine Caban, from Ft. Lauderdale, Florida, practices what she refers to as Tantric Therapy. After working for years as a Spiritual Healer, Counselor and Angel Intuitive, she now integrates Tantra into her work for therapeutic and healing purposes. She also performs various Tantric Ceremonies and Sacred Rituals for men, women and couples. You can learn more about Tantric Therapy at her website: Tantrictherapy.org

e.b. sarver is an author and healer who has been practicing Tantra since 1998, and working as a healer and Tantric guide since 2002. He also uses other healing techniques, including: massage, Reiki, NLP, hypnotherapy, EFT, emotional release and sound healing. He presently resides in the vicinity of Los Angeles, California. You can contact him by email at: tantric.evan@gmail.com

Francis Eliot, from West Yorkshire, U.K., is a healer and life-coach specializing in transformation of behavior and consciousness through methods such as bio-energy healing, 5 Rhythms dance, tantra and raw/living foods. He has completed many trainings and studied with various teachers and meditators including Thich Nhat Hanh, Gabrielle Roth & Byron Katie. He has taught Gabrielle Roth's 5 Rhythms since 2004 and is deeply inspired by the healing power of dance. He is also an active father. You can book a personal consultation with Francis, or read his blog at: www.returntoinnocence.org.uk

Gabriella Hartwell lives on the island of Kauai, Hawaii, is an Intuitive Relationship Life Coach, mentor, and author of the book *You Find Your Soul Mate When You Let Go of Searching*. She offers coaching sessions for singles and couples as well as angel readings and dream interpretations. Visit her website at: www.EmergingSoul.com

Kathleen Ann Staley, from Paradise, California, has deep passion for art and humanity. She writes positive stories about love, hope and world peace. She has six volumes of short stories to date, from Publishamerica. Her fondest desires are to have movies made from her stories, and to travel the world. She plans to continue writing from her heart and soul for the rest of her life. You can contact her at: skittyclark@aol.com, or join her on Facebook at: www.facebook.com/profile.php?id=1679290454

Janet Lessin, Professor of Tantric Studies at the School of Tantra, is Center Holder for the Temple of Tantra, a federally-recognized spiritual institution on Maui, Hawaii. She also heads the World Polyamory Association, which hosts the annual Harbin Hot Springs California Tantra and Polyamory conference (www.schooloftantra.net/worldpolyamoryassociation/conferences/HarbinHotSprings2011/HarbinHotSprings2011.html). Janet has written Polyamory: The Poly-Tantra Lovestyle (www.schooloftantra.net/Store/Books/PolyamoryManyLoves.htm)

Jena Greer, aka Jenasis Free, from Santa Fe, New Mexico is a published poet, philanthropist, philosopher and writer of the movie 2012: The Collective. She lives to CoExist & Assist without exclusion. She is also the founder of Namaste Journey—Etheric Artist (recreating your OBE's and Experiences into tangible work) and KIND: Kindred Inclination for Namastic Development Philanthropy—Ascension Philosophy. Namaste.

Kylie Devi is a writer and activist who works in the healing arts field assisting others to transform trauma into radical self-acceptance, compassionate action and powerful purpose. She is currently working on two books: *Love After Rape* and *Shakti Awake: Recovering the Spirit from Sexual Trauma*. A native New Yorker, she currently lives in Gainesville, Florida and spends most of her time writing, practicing yoga and qigong, organizing art and poetry events and performing spoken word art. You can subscribe to her blog at: www.kyliedevi.com or connect with her on facebook at www.facebook.com/kyliedevi

Lyvea Rose is an astrologer, counselor, and columnist. She has been published on the web, and in newspapers and magazines. She writes horoscopes for the Psychic Club of Australia, and is now working on her first (funny) book about the stars. You can book an in-depth, personal reading and healing with Lyvea, or subscribe to her newsletter/forecasts, at www.lyvearoseastrology.com

Marion Doerflinger is a freelance writer who lives in Columbia, Missouri. His recently published children's book *Daydreaming Daisy* (co-authored with Josephine Kei Lux) may be seen at BarnesandNobel.com and Amazon.com. He has two adult novels under agency contract with a prominent literary agent in California. Marion may be contacted at: mdpoetryman@yahoo.com. He wishes to express gratitude to Nirtana Goodman for help and advice in writing his essay.

As the founder of the Men's Tantra Circle, which meets twice weekly in Los Angeles, **Martin Hannon** moves through every aspect of his life with a sense of pride and masculinity that has been all but lost in our culture today. His presence serves as an inspiration for the potential of all men. One of the greatest issues in relationship today is that modern men and women have been taught to neutralize their "charge"—to become more alike and "get along smoothly". Martin fearlessly invites and guides men to rediscover what it truly is to be a man, and from that place walk authentically in the world and experience the magnificence of Woman. Over the last ten years, Martin has studied Tantra with Bodhi Avinasha, Dawn Cartwright, Rundy Duphiney and Bernie Prior. Furthermore, he has done extensive work and study around re-discovering man's true role in life and relationship with the Men's Division International, where he defined himself as a leader among men. He is also deeply passionate about loving his woman Charu, founder of Embody Tantra, and sharing the wisdom they are discovering together with the world. Check out what Martin offers at: www.MensTantraCircle.com

You can find out more about **Maya Yonika** on her website at: www.ramamaya.com

Nancy Battye's mission is to expand the awareness of how having compassion for ourselves and having compassion for others will not only make our lives happier and more joyful, but it will expand the world to a much higher level of joy. She is a spiritual person who is excited about life, ecstatic about the privilege of being a mother to her incredible children and excited to help others recognize the beauty of who they are and their purpose in life. She's a certified diver, an industrious businesswoman, a pet lover, amateur photographer, athletically inclined and a student of success principles. She lives in British Columbia. You can find out more about her at: www.NancyBattye.com

P. Maya Morgan resides in the Santa Cruz Mountains, California. She is a self-exploring writer, yogini, gardener, mother, kayaker and earth worshiper of all natural beauty, including a lifelong Sierra Club activist/hiker. Many thanks to my Sisters of the Sacred Circle of Santa Cruz for inspiring me to write and for publishing various personal empowerment articles in the *Goddess Circle News*. She is currently in the process of writing stories of her solo travel adventures. P.O. Box 1407, Felton, CA 95018.

Sarah Nolan, from Queensland, Australia, has worked previously in women's health and well-being and is passionate about the empowerment of women and their true higher selves and how this heightens the connection between the masculine and feminine. She is currently in the process of working on her first book.

Sasha Lessin, Ph.D., Dean of Instruction at the School of Tantra (www.schooloftantra.com)certifies professional tantra teachers and trains students and seminar participants how to love each other better. Sasha and wife Janet developed All-Chakra Tantra (www.schooloftantra.net/Store/Books/AllChakraTantra.htm)the comprehensive relationship training program that begins with How To Really Love A Woman: 4 Tantric Trysts (www.schooloftantra.net/Store/Books/HowToReallyLoveAWoman.htm).

Susan A. Kornacki, from Boston, Massachusetts, is an emotional intelligence professional, lifetime experiencer of extraterrestrial energies, and deeply passionate about helping the Earth and mankind through this transition. By far the best job she's held is Mother and friend to her amazing eight year old daughter, Sidney J.

Tantrica Maya is a creative force of nature. She has many talents and gifts with which she has made herself a comfortable life. She is also formally and self-educated in many fields including tantra. As an evolving life artist she chooses to leave herself defined as an open book. Her inspirations carry her along on her life journey. Her main website is www.TheEroticWay.com. You can join her on Facebook by following this link: www.facebook.com/#!/profile.php?id=1535212401

Tracy Uloma Cooper, Ph.D., hails from the Bay Area, and was raised under the teachings of Unity and A Course in Miracles. Previously a counselor with UC Berkeley's Psychological Services department, Tracy's heightened psychological healing as a metaphysician works at the anatomy of a spirit level. Recognizing what makes people really tick and moving to the cause, the true cause, of their imbalances and their weariness with the world...empowering individuals to awaken and author one's own passionate beautiful life! (For newsletter/appointments, e-mail: Tracycoopr@yahoo.com or find her on Facebook: Tracy Cooper ~ The Rose Line)

Soul Rocks is a fresh list that takes the search for soul and spirit mainstream. Chick-lit, young adult, cult, fashionable fiction & non-fiction with a fierce twist.